Nelson Burns

Divine Guidance

Or the Holy Guest

Nelson Burns

Divine Guidance
Or the Holy Guest

ISBN/EAN: 9783337260491

Printed in Europe, USA, Canada, Australia, Japan

Cover: Foto ©Lupo / pixelio.de

More available books at **www.hansebooks.com**

DIVINE GUIDANCE

—OR—

THE HOLY GUEST.

A DISCUSSION
OF THE BELIEVER'S PRIVILEGE
IN CHRIST JESUS. THE HOLY SPIRIT
AS GUIDE INTO ALL TRUTH. THE PENTECOSTAL
BAPTISM. PHYSICAL RELIGIOUS MANIFESTATIONS. INDWELLING
SIN, OR CARNALITY. WHEN AND HOW THE BELIEVER
IS SAVED FROM COMMITTING SIN. MODERN
THEORIES OF ENTIRE SANCTIFICATION.
DIVINE HEALING AND KINDRED
THEMES.

BY

THE REVEREND NELSON BURNS, B.A.,
Gold Medalist of Toronto University.

THE BOOK AND BIBLE HOUSE
BRANTFORD, ONT.
1889.

ENTERED, according to Act of Parliament of Canada, in the year Eighteen hundred and eighty-nine, by THOMAS S. LINSCOTT, in the Office of the Minister of Agriculture.

Publishers' Preface.

WITH more than usual pleasure and satisfaction we present this book to the public. It will doubtless supply a felt need to thousands of Christians, and fill the space that has hitherto been, almost if not quite, a vacuum in modern theology. The book we hope, and confidently expect, will be "a light in a dark place," an emancipator from spiritual doubt and fear, the forerunner of a satisfactory experience, to a vast number of earnest men and women.

The Author possesses no mean literary ability, and after reading this book, one is not surprised to learn that, when a student he captured the gold medal in his class, from the Toronto University. He is also, undoubtedly, as good a man as he is an able writer, and exemplifies in his life the doctrine of "Divine Guidance."

That the book will make a commotion in certain quarters goes without saying; still, even those who do not agree with the views expressed, must admire the candor, the freedom from cant, the logic, and the transparent honesty of the writer. It were too much to say, that this book exhausts the subject of holy living and Divine guidance, and yet it is difficult to see what phase of these questions is not discussed.

We venture the statement, that no true Christian can read this book sympathetically, without having healthful throbs of holy desire, and a mind replenished with additional knowledge of the deep things of God.

Our Author is original in his method of stating Christian truth, and it is really refreshing to read a book in which are found so few hackneyed religious phrases.

The language is simple, and the sentences are short, so that the common people, we trust, will read it gladly; while this is so, there are some burning and profound questions discussed, and conclusions drawn, that, to the man spiritually unlearned, may "be hard to be understood." But we are glad of the words of Jesus, that, "if any man will do His will, he shall know of the doctrine," and there is hope for all who have the child-like spirit in His other statement, "I thank thee, O Father, Lord of heaven and earth, because thou hast hid these things from the wise and prudent, and hast revealed them unto babes." Those, however, who come to this book with a wrong bias, will, we fear, find it like the parables of Jesus were to many of those who waited upon His ministry; and like the truth generally is to those who are not in love with it, "a savour of death unto death." Jesus said to his disciples on one occasion when they were asking him to explain the parable of the sower, "unto you it is given to know the mystery of the kingdom of God; but unto them that are without all these things are done in parables; that seeing they may see and not perceive: and hearing they may hear and not understand." This answer of Jesus seems "a hard saying," and yet it enunciates a principle that is philosophically and historically true. But this part of the Saviour's answer is even more difficult for the unspiritual to understand, than the parable itself, notwithstanding the explanation of the mystery of the parable which follows.

In hearing spiritual truth, especially if it is new to us, we must love the truth absolutely, and possess our souls in patient waiting upon God, or else, the very truth itself, will be a delusion and a snare, and we shall believe a lie and be condemned.

We advise any man, who thinks he cannot be taught more than he knows, concerning Divine guidance, not to read this book; we also extend the same advice to any who are not ready to change their opinions, providing they prove to be incorrect.

To all who hold the truth in righteousness, to all who are in love with Jesus Christ, to all earnest seekers after God, we believe a perusal of this book will be a comfort, an inspiration and a Providential guide.

THE PUBLISHERS.

Author's Preface.

As the first chapter is somewhat introductory in its character, we shall confine ourselves in this short preface to a few explanatory statements.

It was a source of no little satisfaction to us to secure the enterprising publishers, The Book and Bible House, under the management of Rev. T. S. Linscott, to place *Divine Guidance* before the public, seeing we thereby obtained the best facilities we knew of for the accomplishment of our object, which was an extensive circulation of the book. We were somewhat startled when they required our likeness for a frontispiece, but, after consideration, yielded our preference to their superior knowledge concerning this matter.

In Scripture quotations we have uniformly followed the New Version wording when they were taken from the New Testament, but have retained the familiar readings of the Authorized version when selecting from the Old Testament.

THE AUTHOR.

TABLE OF CONTENTS.

CHAP. I.

INTRODUCTION.

Importance of the subject—Hitherto greatly neglected—No standard book on the subject—Indefinite teaching hitherto—Positive teaching—The only satisfactory way—The Author's platform concerning "*all truth*"—Love for the truth necessary—Widespead interest in the subject awakened—Why..17-21

CHAP. II.

THE SCRIPTURAL ARGUMENT.

A Bible doctrine—Not a new doctrine—History of Divine guidance—Adam—Abel—Enoch—Abram—Moses—The central truth of the Mosaic dispensation—Prophets—Their place in this connection—Saul and Samuel, an incident—The heathen world still under the Patriarchal dispensation—David's exploits at Keilah—Use of the ephod—Guidance clear and explicit.............. 22-30

CHAP. III.

DIVINE GUIDANCE BETTER UNDER THE NEW THAN THE OLD DISPENSATION.

Defective nature of the Mosaic dispensation—In what the improvement consists—Recognized by Paul—The Spirit to supersede all laws—The prophetic order ended—Difficulties under the former—Examples, Hazael, Ahab—Removed in the present dispensation... .31-34

CHAP. IV.

THE GUIDANCE OF THE SPIRIT EVEN BETTER THAN THE PERSONAL PRESENCE OF CHRIST.

The advantages of Christ's personal presence—Admitted by Himself—But said that the Spirit's presence would be still better—This dispensation the best of all—Christ's second coming not to be an improvement on it. ....`........35-39

CHAP. V.

CHRIST'S WORDS MORE FULLY CONSIDERED.

They measure its importance — No appeal from them — Incidental illustration — Remarks — All of John's words on the subject quoted — Remarks — Incompleteness explained by Pentecost — The Spirit to be the only guide 40-45

CHAP. VI.

THE PROMISE FULFILLED.

Exact fulfilment of promises — Not only general, but particular — The Holy Ghost now practically ignored — Not so with the early Christians — This fact explains their writings — Example, letter to the Galatians — Corinthians — Several passages with explanations — Incidental illustrations of Divine guidance — Ethiopian eunuch — Barnabas and Saul — Paul and Silas — Guidance always connected in their thought with the Pentecostal gift — Their confidence in the Spirit's work 46-56

CHAP. VII.

THE TRUE ARGUMENT.

Bible only can establish the doctrine — Practice of modern Christians not a safe argument — A revealed truth — Stands or falls with divinity of Christ — *Conscious* guidance — Apostles knew the Spirit was guiding them — Advantages of positive, definite knowledge 57-61

CHAP. VIII.

WHAT IS DIVINE GUIDANCE?

Izaak Walton's advice — What shall we do with the doctrine of Divine Guidance? — Definition of Divine guidance — A felt want — Should meet this fully — To walk worthy of God requires guidance — How guided of secondary importance — A matter of curiosity — Better to learn by experience 62-68

CHAP. IX.

THE MANNER OF DIVINE GUIDANCE

Phantom-like notions about guidance — Guidance in Abraham's time and ours compared — Extraordinary phenomena discussed and their place assigned — Witness to sins forgiven, argument therefrom .. 69-73

CHAP. X.

THE MANNER OF DIVINE GUIDANCE, CONTINUED.

Perfect faith necessary—Efforts to limit the Spirit's work—A sign of unbelief—Willingness the outcome of confidence—Impressions—Incident in life of Dr. Bangs—Impressional guidance not Divine guidance—Dreams, visions, etc.—Use of the Bible—Reason—Common sense—In harmony with the Bible and reason................74-81

CHAP. XI.

THE EXTENT OF DIVINE GUIDANCE.

Incidental illustrations—Reasons for giving personal experience—History of an impression—How to judge righteous judgment—Examples—An imperfect Christian..82-87

CHAP. XII.

INCIDENTAL ILLUSTRATIONS CONTINUED.

An incident in pastoral work—Can we know when to visit and when not?—A street-car incident—When is a matter great or small?—An eye lost—In a railroad accident—No line dividing secular and sacred..88-96

CHAP. XIII.

THE DOCTRINE OF DIVINE GUIDANCE IN ITS SCOPE.

Not the gift of the Holy Ghost, but almost synonymous with it—Ignoring it accounts for unsatisfactory longings—These very general—A fundamental doctrine—The lesson of Toulon—The first bestowment confined to the 120—Character of the 120—What they were waiting for—Nature of the ten days' delay—Not to be repeated—Signs and wonders, why given—Not permanent—What was permanent—"The place was shaken," etc., exposition of this passage—Gift of the Holy Ghost the permanent characteristic of this dispensation—Two kinds of disciples—Second blessing.............97-110

CHAP. XIV.

THE GIFT OF THE SPIRIT NECESSARILY IMPLIES COMPLETE GUIDANCE.

This gift a *person*—Meaning of walking in the Spirit—Rejection of the doctrine accounts for a low Christian experience—Faith—Illustrations—Acting faith—Faith the result of careful examination. 111-118

CHAP. XV.

SIMPLICITY RESTORED.

Mysticism--Antinomianism—The result of ignoring Pentecost—Antinomianism in many holiness creeds—Why.................119-125

CHAP. XVI.

CARNALITY.

The forgiven sinner ready for heaven—Practically taught by all—Wesley's theory examined—The weak part of holiness creeds—A solution—Explains seventh and eighth chapters of Romans.........126-132

CHAP. XVII.

CARNALITY, CONTINUED.

Cleansing or heart purity—Another name for a righteous life—Means more than this in some theologies—An object lesson—This thought examined—These questions not raised in apostolic times—Sanctification and entire sanctification—Distinction not scriptural or logical—Love and perfect love—Confusion caused by their present way of being used—Hitherto an unsolved problem—An object lesson—A proposed way to meet the difficulty—Fitful obedience and continued obedience 133-145

CHAP. XVIII.

SCRIPTURALNESS OF THIS TEACHING.

Doctrines based on *few* and *many* scriptures contrasted—Table showing number of times different expressions are used—Examination of the scriptures concerning cleansing—Indefinite teaching in them all—Definite teaching in those which refer to the Holy Ghost—Satisfactory result of the comparison 146-155

CHAP. XIX.

TEMPTATIONS.

Without and within theory examined—Keeping the Sabbath—A modernized testimony as an object lesson—Temptations of Christ—First temptation--Second—Third—Origin of the nomenclature—Not scriptural—Should be ruled out 156-166

CHAP. XX.

MISTAKES AND INFIRMITIES.

In a chaotic state—The scapegoat of modern holiness creeds—These creeds generalized—Their weak points—The *Gordian knot*, how cut—Completely met in Divine guidance—How to vitiate a profession of holiness—Mistakes—Different shades of meaning—The true scriptural meaning...167-175

CHAP. XXI.

PRAYER AND SCRIPTURE STUDY.

Antagonism between the legalistic and spiritual—Two classes—Why they opposed Christ—Defending their acts—The *within kingdom*—Explanation of antagonism—Peter as a legalist—When given up—Two ways—No satisfaction in the one—Complete satisfaction in the other—Times and seasons for prayer, etc., when may they be given up?...176-187

CHAP. XXII.

THE LAW OF THE SPIRIT AND THE DRESS QUESTION.

Present confusion in teaching—Needs to be regulated by this law—Scriptural teaching examined—Two canons on the subject—The teaching which is generally accepted—Teaching and practice not in harmony—Gold in this connection—Modern teaching makes Peter contradict himself—Aaron's dress—Israelites at Sinai—The lilies—The true adornment—Limited application of scripture texts—Women teaching—Dr. Johnson's opinion on dress—The argument of expense—Personal experience—Object of this discussion............188-201

CHAP. XXIII.

PHYSICAL MANIFESTATIONS.

What holiness is—Essentials and non-essentials—The *normal* Christian state—An illustrative incident—Origin of such incidents—Mistakes concerning spiritual joy—Fresh baptisms a sign of human origin—Counterfeits, how recognized—The true baptism, how known.202-211

CHAP. XXIV.

DIVINE GUIDANCE AND THE CARE OF OUR BODIES.

Being led of the Spirit secures all possible benefits for the body—True for communities—And for individuals—According to the judgment of Christ—The words of Christ—Their meaning—Is sickness the proof of the presence of sin?—Set rules concerning healing not a part of the spiritual kingdom—Attitude to the Divine healing movement —No need for their rule of health—Not in the epistles—The words of James examined—Healing classed with miracles—Promises confined to Israelites—Healing not for all.....................212-230

CHAP. XXV.

OBJECTIONS CONSIDERED.

Frankly considered—Should have the benefit of every doubt—INFALLIBILITY—No danger in real guidance, but in false guidance—The spirit of infallibility largely prevalent—The best antidote—Absence of Divine guidance the real danger—The word a misnomer—*Thus saith the Lord*, its value considered—DEPRECIATING THE BIBLE—Regulates Bible authority—Results of making the Bible the only guide—Bible taxed beyond its ability—Paul's writings concerning women teaching compared with other scriptures—Testimonies concerning neglecting their Bibles examined 231-244

CHAP. XXVI.

OBJECTIONS, CONTINUED.

LAWLESSNESS—Awakens fears—Chained lions—God the author of law cannot lead into lawlessness—Imitations—The guards against this —Object is to keep law—DANGERS—Too dangerous to meddle with —The origin of this dread—Misunderstanding the Spirit's character and work—Thomas Walsh—Wesley's opinion—The only antidote— Special guards for the Spirit's work—The Holy Ghost same in character as Christ—UNCHRISTIANIZING OTHERS—Men judged according to their light—Love for truth—John Wesley with his Bible—His state before conversion—The attitude towards light all-important— A CHECK ON INDUSTRY—Holy Spirit not a servant—When labor is best that will be the manner of Divine Guidance............245-257

CHAP. XXVII.

LIVING TESTIMONY.

Reasons for them 258-259

THE CHRISTIAN EXPERIENCE OF REV. B. SHERLOCK.

Brought up religiously—Converted at 15—A few years after perfected in love—Did not last—Why—Resolutions not part of God's plan—Obtained and lost the blessing many times—Wrote letters in *Guardian* on the subject—One of the founders of the Canada Holiness Association—History of Association work—Holy Spirit sole cause of holiness—Baptized into the Holy Ghost—Guidance of the Spirit—Now complete satisfaction—Constantly guided—Increased usefulness...259-265

CHRISTIAN EXPERIENCE OF ISAAC ANDERSON.

Object of the writer—Born near Galt—Education limited—First effort to be a Christian—First visit to a church at the age of 13—Converted after a severe conflict—Joins the church—A life of sinning and repenting—Came to Toronto, 1870—Finally restored, 1880—Led into blessing of holiness—Perpetual cleansing—Joseph Cook's works—How to lead a justified life—The only Holiness meeting in the city—How to live a holy *business life*—The secret found—How business is done—Domestic afflictions—God's grace sufficient........265-275

CHRISTIAN EXPERIENCE OF MRS. McMAHON.

Born near Lake Ontario—The power of God realized—The dawning of spiritual knowledge—The beginning of spiritual conflict—Early love for Christ, followed by conflict—Nature of this conflict—Church work—An enigma—Sorrows and their result—Study of the work of the Spirit—New Year's consecration—Failure—The remedy—Clear light—Rest secured—Its description.....................275-281

CHRISTIAN EXPERIENCE OF REV. A. TRUAX.

Conversion clear—Prayer to "stay His hand"—Comparative failure—The blessing of perfect love—How obtained—Disappointment—How to know the will of God the question—Grimsby Park—Cry for *certain knowledge*—The fight of faith—Victory..............281-284

THE CHRISTIAN EXPERIENCE OF J. K. CRANSTON.

Converted during the great revival at Galt—At Port Hope—At Woodstock—In business at Galt—Experience not satisfactory—Experience of other Christians the same—Mr. Caldwell's experience—Close examination thereof—Helpful experience of others—Receiving the Comforter...284-288

DIVINE GUIDANCE.

CHAPTER I.

Howbeit when He, the Spirit of truth, is come, He shall guide you into all truth.—John xvi. 13.

THE office of the third person in the Divine Trinity which is indicated by the promise of Jesus, "He shall guide you into all truth," is of supreme importance in its relation to man.

And yet, whilst the practical value of this attitude of "The Father's co-eternal Paraclete" can scarcely be exaggerated, no part of the redemptive scheme has been so carelessly examined, or so completely ignored.

Over a score of years ago, the writer remarked to a brother minister, "The book on Divine guidance has yet to be written," and still this statement is true. So, in striving to meet this need, we are conscious of exploring a *terra incognita*, as far as other book writers are concerned.

True it is that here and there a chapter, in some work on the Higher Life, promises the searcher after truth some definite help. But, like the mirage of the desert, the promise and its fulfilment are separated by infinite distances.

We mean, that no definite, positive teaching concerning the word *all* in the promise of Christ can be found in any of the writings on this subject.

For instance, no writer takes the position that all in the representative passage above quoted means every truth without limitation, nor, on the other hand, that it means no truth whatever.

Hence they are forced to make it mean *some* truths. But they fail to give a clear, distinct division, showing, on the one hand, what truths it does mean, and on the other hand, what it does not include in its apparently comprehensive scope; and hence, of pure necessity, they leave the whole subject where they found it, plus the mystery resulting from their inconsequential reasonings.

We crave the patience of the reader at this point, asking to be borne with in re-stating this matter, because of a seeming censure on others, and an implied superiority on the part of the present writer.

It is our design to investigate this subject after an exhaustive manner, to secure, if possible, definite, positive views concerning it. Now, but very little thought must make it evident to all that no *definite* creed can be formulated, unless *all* in the promise of Christ is made to mean either *every* truth or *no* truth. But as all Christian writers, who have hitherto written on this question, have adopted neither of these extremes, it follows that no clear, definite creed could be formulated by them concerning the whole subject.

For, as before intimated, the absolute necessity devolved on them of dividing all truths into what would come within the province of this promise, and what would not.

But this task, manifestly, cannot be performed short of a direct revelation. The revelation is omitted in the Bible, hence it is beyond the possible as far as these or any other writers are concerned.

Therefore it is self-evident, that all writers who commence or continue to write on this subject, on the assumption that *all truth* in this statement of the Saviour means only *some truth*, must inevitably come short of clear, definite teaching concerning the whole doctrine of Divine guidance.

Now as we, without hesitation, take the extreme view of the passage which maintains that "all truth" means all truth without limitation as to time, place or quantity, that the promise carries its face value, we suggest, that however startled the reader may be by this announcement, if he should turn away from investigation along this positive line—he turns away from the only possible solution of this problem of the ages.

We submit, therefore, that our extreme platform can confidently invite the careful investigation of every genuine truth-lover, not only because of its promises concerning truth ultimate in this direction, but because of the absolute certainty of its being found in no other direction.

If the frank, unmistakable statement of our creed on this vital question, at the very beginning of our writings, should deter some from venturing with us to examine freely the whole subject, we believe it will arrest the attention of all to the fact, that at the least we hold the courage of our convictions, and therefore leave no room for temptations to conceal our real sentiments, or hide them behind reasonings many or multiplied verbiage.

But we demand in this investigation what may startle still more, and mayhap deter the inveterate curiosity-seeker from further perusal of the book. For we maintain that a genuine love of the truth, as truth, must characterize him who would investigate successfully this subject; a truth-loving spirit that will evince its genuineness by gladly and recklessly incorporating into the life whatsoever appears, on mature investigation, to have the imprimatur of Christ—the embodiment of truth—on it.

For we are possessed with the conviction that all others, whether cursory readers or close students of these chapters, will rise from their investigation with unsatisfied longings.

Like as the fabled ivory gates of fairy land are said to refuse to open to him whose soul is not pure and free from stain, so the golden gate into the knowledge of the truth as it is in Jesus refuses to respond to the touch of him who cannot from the heart say to the great Captain of our salvation, " Lord, I will follow Thee whithersoever Thou goest."

Hence our investigation must proceed along the line, not of curiosity, but of earnest quest after truth—truth to be embraced and lived out in the life so soon as all reasonable demands of the soul concerning its genuineness are met.

Let not then the reader be surprised if we approach this subject after a sort unexpected and unusual. For our first effort shall be, not to meet the many objections that on every hand are urged against this extreme teaching, but to examine Scripture utterance, as if examining authoritative, dogmatic teaching concerning this thing.

Certainly we do not ignore the patent fact that almost every writer of note, who is known in the religious world as a specialist on the subject of holiness, has taken up his parable against our views on this theme, and has attempted to refute them.

But this fact, to the thoughtful mind, in place of being a *prima facie* evidence of our position being a false one, furnishes some proof for the contrary thought. That is, it is evidence that it is because of conscious lack of definite belief in this direction that such visible agitation, in the minds of the ablest writers, has been evinced.

For if one with our antecedents and surroundings had antagonized any one truth of general acceptance—a truth, we remark, whose dimensions and results were fully understood and defined—how utterly impossible for him to attract attention further than a passing remark, embodying pity or contempt. That such widespread attention has been aroused to the subject of the guidance of the Holy Spirit, can only be explained on the assumption that this truth is of vital importance, and that the views held by even our foremost writers on the subject are loose and uncertain. All of which is our excuse, not only for striving to gain the ear of the public, but also for asking that attention sufficiently long to study the subject of Divine guidance thoroughly.

CHAPTER II.

THE SCRIPTURAL ARGUMENT.

To the law and the testimony: if they speak not according to this word, it is because there is no light in them.—Isaiah viii. 20.

THAT the Holy Spirit was promised as guide during the Gospel dispensation is admitted by all readers of the Bible. So, at first sight, it seems like wasting needlessly the time of the reader in dealing with argument or Scripture reference to establish a universally received truth. And yet, when we come to the full consideration of the word *all*, it will be found needful, for our *continued* belief in the general truth, to realize on what a solid foundation it rests.

The fact of being guided after a supernatural way, is not a new thought, for the first time mentioned in the New Testament, or as being confined to the Gospel dispensation.

As a matter of history, it occupies a very prominent place in all preceding dispensations.

Immediately after the fall of our first parents, sacred history represents the guilty pair as having direct communication with the Divine mind, and during this interview they received definite instructions suited to their present needs.

So, too, both Cain and Abel had intercourse with Heaven—Abel learning, of a certainty, that his sacrifice was accepted of God, and Cain, that his was rejected.

Of Enoch, it is narrated that he walked with God, and that walk, not to be meaningless, must imply direct intercourse between the two.

Noah distinctly obtained the mind of God, not only concerning general truth, but also concerning minute details in preparing his ark of safety.

In the same way Abram had communication with the invisible Jehovah, and so firm was his belief in this fact, that he shaped his whole life to accord with this belief. Not, we again remark, his general belief in God, but his definite faith in the fact that he personally received communications from God.

In the days of Moses, this general belief that God occasionally communicated with individual man, was established as the great central truth of the Jewish Church. The fact was insisted on, that there would always be a class of men to whom God would communicate sufficient knowledge for the passing needs of the nation, as a whole, and for each individual thereof. This knowledge was to be given to such prophets as would, from time to time, be raised up, until Messiah should come.

Minute instructions and rules were given whereby the people might recognize, and follow the true prophets, and detect, and reject the false.

But notice well the fact, that all were not priests or prophets. But all might have access to God, through them, to learn His mind, both in national and individual matters, whether sacred or secular.

What more secular matter could be brought before God, through His prophet, than the straying away of the asses of Kish? And yet we find Saul, as a matter of course, inquiring of Samuel concerning this ordinary, secular matter, plainly indicating thereby the general custom of the day. We find, too, that Samuel received him without rebuke and fully met him in this his wish.

True it is that weightier matters, of national importance, were connected with his visit to Samuel, at that time; but of these we speak not now, for they, in no way, detract from the thought we are here making prominent, viz., that it was the privilege of any Jew to find out a prophet of the Lord, and inquire of God, at his mouth, concerning any matter, whether sacred or secular, which affected him as an individual.

That is, whilst the Israelite had the written law, and the sacrificial institutions of Moses, they had in no sense impaired or lessened the advantages of the Patriarchal dispensation. Men were still raised up, who, like Abraham, Jacob, or Moses, could have direct communication with Heaven, and be a channel of communication for others. Nay, in this matter there was apparently a decided improvement upon former times.

The heathen world still under the Patriarchal dispensation.—It may seem like turning aside from sober argument to the enchanting fields of speculation, to suggest, at this point, that the simplest explanation of God's government of the world is in the thought that, before Pentecost, all who did not come under the influence of Judaism, still remained under the Patriarchal dispensation; and that still it is true, that all who hear not the Gospel, have assured to them—in their relations to God and one another—all the advantages that existed in the times of Nahor and Laban.

But the leading thought of this chapter is, that individual men had distinct audience with Deity in all the dispensations of grace up to the time of the ushering in of the New, last dispensation. And further, that the outcome of those communications with Heaven was positive guidance in matters temporal as well as spiritual.

Need we transform ourselves into a concordance here, for the convenience of our readers, and burden the text with numerous, quoted verses of the Bible? We believe the memories of most readers will more pleasantly accomplish this task.

Direct Divine guidance is brought out in a multitude of passages, as incidents in the lives of Scripture worthies. To simply mention such names as Abraham, Jacob, Joseph, Moses, Joshua, Manoah, Samuel, Saul, David, Jonathan, and a host of others, causes these incidents to flash before the mind's eye, in bright panoramic vision, until the long procession of events of this character seems like a glowing stream of Heaven's own brightness forging its way through all the dark past, till it is lost in the exceeding glory of Pentecost.

But we yield to the temptation of prolonging the view at one point, and ask lengthened attention to the incident connected with David's exploits at Keilah.

It was whilst David was in hiding with a few hundred men from the army of Saul, that he heard of the Philistines making military raids on his countrymen at Keilah, and distressing them with all the calamities of petty warfare.

Now David was a patriot of the highest type, and this news aroused him to forgetfulness of his own perilous situation and to an eager desire to succour his distressed countrymen, and so, with that reckless valor which characterized him, he resolved to go to their help.

But whilst David was a man of war, and a true patriot, above all he was a man of God. That is, however, obscured at times, the religious element in him was the highest of all motives. Hence he checked his fiery impulse sufficiently to inquire of God as to whether or no he should go.

The narrative is short and simple, and goes not into details as to how he talked with God. But this is suggestive of the fact, that it was not considered, in those days, an extraordinary matter for any man, under peculiar circumstances, to inquire of God concerning his life work.

And let it be well remembered here, that David's claims to being a prophet were by no means then fully recognized. This is shown by the fact, that his followers objected to the expedition, and with apparently good reasons. "And David's men said unto him, Behold, we be afraid here in Judah; how much more, then, if we come to Keilah against the armies of the Philistines?"

Now this reasoning, on the part of his men, seemed to be unanswerable from the standpoint of reason and common sense. Accordingly, David did not stay to meet it after the modern pattern, for it is added, "Then David inquired of the Lord yet again. And the Lord answered him and said, Arise, go down to Keilah: for I will deliver the Philistines into thine hand."

And now it appears from the story, that their objections were fully met, solely on the ground that in some way God had made known to them, through David, the fact that the expedition would be both safe and successful.

But again they are in a dilemma. Tidings are brought that Saul is coming against them. Two courses are now open to them, viz., to remain and resist Saul behind the walls of the city, or to take refuge in flight.

It would seem that the first method had the preference in their thoughts. But there was one element of uncertainty connected with the matter. The inhabitants of Keilah, however grateful to-day, when they should see that to espouse the cause of David might prove the destruction of their city, might falter in their loyalty to him, turn traitors in the time of battle, and so betray David and his men into the hands of their enemies.

Evidently, this was a matter no amount of reasoning could settle, for even if the professions of the people, as to their willingness to stand by their protectors, were sincere and honest, it would not follow that they would not fail them in the time of real danger, through fear. Hence, the narrative goes on to say, that again David sought the mind of God in his perplexity, and again he was met by definite replies to all his questions.

But in this case there were more formalities used, or at all events mentioned, for Abiathar, the priest, in the meantime, had joined his company, having with him an *ephod*. Hence, we are informed, that David now recognized him as the *via media* of approach to God, according to the laws of Moses, and in the use of the prescribed means he secured the Divine direction he so much desired.

And notice, that the communications from God were

clear and explicit. "And he said to Abiathar the priest, Bring hither the ephod. Then said David, O Lord God of Israel, thy servant hath certainly heard that Saul seeketh to come to Keilah, to destroy the city for my sake. Will the men of Keilah deliver me up into his hand? Will Saul come down as thy servant hath heard? O Lord God of Israel, I beseech thee tell thy servant. And the Lord said, He will come down. Then said David, Will the men of Keilah deliver me and my men into the hands of Saul? And the Lord said, They will deliver thee up."

We draw especial attention to the clear-cut nature of these questions and answers, and to the implicit faith in them of all concerned. There was no hesitation on the part of David and his men in acting on them. No speculations concerning the nature of the business in hand, as to whether it was sacred or secular, seemed to interfere with their prompt action, and no doubts rent the band in sunder. They simply acted as if it was an ordinary matter. God had been appealed to, in their difficulty, in the appointed way, and His reply settled the whole matter.

Now this, we maintain, is a well authenticated and circumstantially related specimen of Divine guidance under the former dispensation. But it is clearly revealed that the old is done away. True, but it is as clearly stated both by prophet and apostle, yea, by Christ Himself, that it was in order to give place to something better.

Hence our argument, that whatever Divine guidance may or may not be, at the present time, any representation thereof which, in practical advantages to us as individuals, does not measure up to and far surpass those enjoyed in David's times, cannot, in the nature of the case, be all that is warranted by the teaching of Scripture.

Then, too, in all parts of the Bible, how vividly is the fact of Divine guidance brought out in rapturous utterance, whether of fervent prayer for guidance, or thanksgiving for guidance received. "Thou wilt guide me with Thy counsel." "The steps of a good man are ordered by the Lord." "The meek will He guide in judgment." "Commit thy way unto the Lord, trust also in Him, and He shall bring it to pass." "He will give His angels charge over thee, to keep thee in all thy ways." "*He* guided them in the wilderness like a flock." "And guided them by the skilfulness of His hands." "Thou in thy mercy hast led forth the people which thou hast redeemed: thou hast guided them in thy strength unto thy holy habitation." These, it will be readily admitted, are but specimens of a vast number of similar passages.

And here, too, the element of definiteness is not wanting, but runs, like a golden thread, through all generalities. Indeed, many of the rhapsodies of the Old Testament are founded, like those of Moses and Deborah on the banks of the Red Sea, on instances of distinct, definite Divine guidance.

Thus is made evident, even to the cursory reader of the Old Testament, the fact that the doctrine of Divine guidance was not only accepted as part of the old dispensations, but was made to do practical service in the life-work of the saints of every age. And moreover, we see that this consisted not merely of some general recognition of a Divine superintendence of them and their life-work, but was known as a distinct element in their lives, as positive to them as the intuitions of their intellect. And, further, they followed these intimations of God with even greater confidence than the instincts and operations of their minds.

CHAPTER III.

DIVINE GUIDANCE BETTER UNDER THE NEW THAN UNDER THE OLD DISPENSATION.

THERE are many prophetic utterances which distinctly point to a vast practical improvement in this matter in the New Dispensation.

Moses, after he had completed the work given him to do, seemed to realize its defective nature, and promised the world that another, and *last* prophet would be raised up, who would complete the work he had in hand, and usher in a perfected dispensation.

"I will put my law in their inward parts and write it in their hearts. . . . And they shall teach no more every man his neighbor, and every man his brother, saying, Know the Lord; for they shall all know me, from the least of them unto the greatest of them, saith the Lord."—Jer. xxxi. 33.

Here a contrast evidently is instituted, implying that there was to be a vast superiority, in the matter of knowing the mind of God, in the New Dispensation, as compared with the Old.

This contrast was to be seen in two respects, viz., concerning the written law, and concerning the communications from God through His prophets.

In the one case, the laws of God, engraven on brass and stone, or written on other material, are evidently contrasted with some intuitional or heart knowledge of the will of God concerning us.

Of course all the advantages and disadvantages of a written code of laws were fully known to the prophet, and yet he foretells something vastly superior to these things with which they were familiar and as distinctly contrasted therewith.

And mark, that this contrast could scarcely be fulfilled by simply subtracting some of the old, cancelled laws, and adding others in their place, as is the teaching of many, for the prophet more than suggests a radical change in the manner of knowing the mind of God.

This contrast was fully recognized by the Apostle Paul, in the eighth and ninth chapters of his letter to the Hebrews, in a passage too lengthy for quotation here, but which will repay the reader for a close study in this connection. For it will be noticed that the writer took it for granted that his readers understood this contrast as indicated, and so he argued on that assumption.

But in the third chapter of his second epistle to the Corinthians, he uses the same figure of contrast in a somewhat modified form, and likens the influence of his Corinthian converts on the world around them to the work of the Holy Spirit in their heart. "Ye are our epistle written in our hearts, known and read of all men. Forasmuch as ye are manifestly declared to be the epistle of Christ ministered by us, written not with ink, but with the Spirit of the living God; not in tablets of stone, but in fleshly tables of the heart."

Here Paul evidently has reference to the prophecy under consideration, and contrasts the Spirit's work as teacher or guide in this dispensation, with the written law of former times, in two ways, first by the fact that they, his converts, by their Christian testimony and consistent lives, unlike the dead letter of the law, appealed, as living teachers, directly to them in all the warmth of personal contact; and second, that his conscious or heart-knowledge of them as his children in the Gospel contrasted with cold intellectual knowledge, even as the knowledge which comes directly from the Spirit contrasts with that which is the outcome of the study of the written law.

Paul emphasizes the position for which we are contending, viz., that prophecy, in contrasting the old dispensation with the new, concerning Divine guidance, plainly predicted that the Holy Spirit, as guide into all truth, would supersede all laws whether human or Divine, and be to each and every one, so receiving him, the law of God, written on his heart, so that he might know God, and the things freely given to him of God.

And secondly, this was to do away with the cumbersome prophetic order. In the old dispensation it was necessary either to be a prophet oneself, or to find out a prophet, in order to "know the Lord," that is, find out the mind of God concerning the things which affected the individual either in his single or corporate capacity. But all could not be prophets. And there were false as well as true prophets. Hence, manifestly, there were possibilities of failure in obtaining the mind of God which could not be ignored.

Hazael, as messenger from his master, the King of Damascus, to Elijah, obtained the mind of God concerning the king's sickness, but the king, through the servant's treachery, failed to know and profit thereby.

Ahab, although he obtained the true word of the Lord from one prophet, was perplexed by the confident contrary utterances of numerous false prophets.

And so, when wicked kings, or worldly-minded prophets ruled the land, they filled the Lord's description of the Scribes and Pharisees—" Ye entered not in yourselves, and them that were entering in ye hindered."

But, by contrast, this whole machinery of approach to God is swept away in Christ, who has sent the Spirit to wait on every child of God, and by personal, direct communication, guide him into all truth so that, as prophet, he need not teach the people, saying, " Know ye the Lord," nor, as searching for one of the Lord's prophets, need he inquire amongst his neighbours, " Know ye the Lord?" in order to inquire of the Lord at his mouth. For the grand contrasted picture is, " All shall know Me, from the least even to the greatest."

Now let this glorious contrast be kept in mind, and it pours such a flood of light on the prophecies concerning this thing that we wonder not at the strong language of Paul when, beholding this wondrous disparity, he exclaims, " The former had no glory by reason of the glory that excelleth."

CHAPTER IV.

THE GUIDANCE OF THE SPIRIT EVEN BETTER THAN THE PERSONAL PRESENCE OF CHRIST.

OUR Saviour not only endorsed this view of the case, but taught that Divine guidance, on and after Pentecost, would exceed in advantages even the short dispensation when He Himself was present with His disciples. "It is expedient for you that I go away, for if I go not away the Comforter will not come to you; but if I go away I will send Him unto you."—John xvi. 7.

Now Jesus proclaimed Himself to be the light of the world, as having all power, not only to interpret all laws—human and Divine—in their relation to individual man, but even to annul them when needful. "In this place is one greater than the Sabbath."

Now, from this His power to instruct and guide into ultimate truth, His disciples secured all possible benefit. For He did not confine Himself, in His ministry to them, to giving such general truths as are found in the sermon on the Mount, but also interested Himself in the minute details of every-day life, as witness His direction to Peter to catch the fish which would furnish the sum needed to pay their tribute money.

Moreover, He endeared Himself to them by the magnetism of a full-orbed friendship, until Peter only voiced the attachment of all when he declared he could die for

Him. From this impulsive utterance of Peter and the ready endorsation of the sentiment by the others, as well as by other expressions in the Gospels, we are led to believe that the disciples to a great extent appreciated the advantages of their close relations to the Messiah. Hence, when He spoke of leaving them, they evinced genuine sorrow of heart: "Because I have said these things unto you, sorrow hath filled your heart."

And Jesus evidently did not discount this their grief, or minify the cause of it. No tricks of voluntary humility prevented Him from frankly admitting the great value of His personal presence with them. He acknowledges it all: "Ye call me Lord and Master, and ye say well, for so I am."

And yet with this full recognition on the part of all of the great, the inestimable blessings which the disciples possessed by the visible presence of their Master, Christ taught them that the advent of "the Comforter, which is the Holy Ghost," to abide with them and to guide them into all truth, would be such an improvement upon all former blessings, that on the whole it would be better for them that He should leave them. "Nevertheless, I tell you the truth. It is expedient for you that I go away, for if I go not away the Comforter will not come unto you, but if I go I will send Him unto you."

Therefore we contend that the doctrine of Divine guidance, as a vital part of the New Covenant, must take a form in practical life, not only to measure up to and surpass all possible privileges in this respect under the Old Testament dispensation, but must even exceed the privileges enjoyed by Matthew and John during the three years' ministry of our Lord on earth.

And as might be expected from such a teacher, this thought runs through many of His expressions. For, in His allusions to the future gift of the Holy Ghost, He seemed always to imply something of good surpassing the possibilities of His own times.

Hear Him cry in the audience of all the people, "He that believeth on Me, as the Scripture hath said, out of his belly shall flow rivers of living water." And this He said, in the spirit of prophecy, concerning the coming of the Holy Ghost, as is carefully remarked by the evangelist. Certainly this carries the mind of the hearer forward to something still better in the future.

John the Baptist, as narrated by all four evangelists, proclaimed the chief end of the coming of Christ to be that He might make it possible for the Holy Ghost to come and abide in the world in some fuller sense than ever before.

"In *that day* ye shall know that I am in my Father and ye in me and I in you." The day of Pentecost, here alluded to, was to be to them the real revelation of Himself, for until that time their eyes were to be holden that they should not fully know Him.

Again after His resurrection, when first he met with them, in the inner room, the doors being shut, He breathed on them and said, "Receive ye the Holy Ghost." As if to remind them that not His death, however necessary in the grand redemption scheme, not His resurrection glory, however essential as proving to them His divinity and their sure hope of a coming resurrection, either single or unitedly, were of such importance to them as the great coming event which would take place in the near future.

And as a confirmation of this view we point to the fact that all His teachings continually were, as so many finger boards, pointing to that grand event which would complete the scheme of redemption, and fit them not only to be partners of His joy, but also to be efficient co-workers with Him in gathering together out of all kindreds a people to His name.

Strange that with this plain statement of Christ as to the superiority of the reign of the Holy Ghost, any still should build their hopes of the triumph of Christianity on any coming dispensation as superior to the present.

For certainly it would leave the words of Christ when describing the advent of the Spirit to complete His work meaningless, if His coming again in His bodily presence to this world would usher in a still better dispensation of grace.

Does not the sighing for something further awaken the suspicion that the full glory of this, the Spirit's day, has not yet been realized, and are we certain that Paul would not meet these expectations with the question, "Have ye received the Holy Ghost since ye believed?"

But, not to pursue this thought farther, we recur to the leading argument of the chapter. Christ himself did teach that the doctrine of Divine guidance was to take to itself a new significance that would enhance its practical value to man far beyond what it was in former dispensations. Indeed He implied in His teachings a minuteness of guidance which exhausts language to express.

How else explain His instructions concerning care for the body, concerning the government of thought, even under such trying circumstances as when arraigned before the tribunals of earth, with the death penalty as the outcome of failure on our part to make a good defence? How do the will of God on earth as it is done in heaven unless provision be made for knowing momentarily what that good and perfect will of God is? How be perfect as our Father in heaven is perfect, unless the Holy Spirit shall have right of way in our being and thus make possible every requirement of God moment by moment through successive years? How, in fine, make good Christ's claim that His "yoke is easy and His burden light," when He demands that we judge our lives by such sublime standards, if some arrangement does not co-exist with His commands whereby we may have intuitional power to know the will of God in all particulars as it affects us, as well as have the ability to perform that which is revealed to us?

To leave out this part of the plan of salvation would loosen the very foundation of the superstructure, and speedily bring the whole building of God, consisting of commands, denunciations and promises, to the ground in one indistinguishable mass of useless ruin.

CHAPTER V.

CHRIST'S WORDS MORE FULLY CONSIDERED.

BUT manifestly the words of the last teacher of ultimate truth, the man Christ Jesus, must measure the importance and extent of the doctrine of guidance through the Holy Ghost.

Hence it is absolutely necessary to examine carefully and minutely all His teachings on this subject, with the full understanding that there is no appeal from them. Neither prophet nor apostle can be made to occupy any place higher than illustrator or enforcer of His utterances.

Now, whilst all four evangelists mention John the Baptist's declaration concerning Jesus as He who should baptize with the Holy Ghost, Luke and John are the ones who more minutely narrate Christ's teaching concerning the gift and work of the Spirit.

The reason of this is obvious, for Matthew and Mark seem to have confined themselves to the works and teachings of Christ as they affected the people at the time. Their histories suddenly close at the resurrection, with just a few words of His final counsels and directions to the eleven disciples, Matthew not even mentioning the fact of the ascension.

But with Luke and John the case is very different. For Luke continues the history of Christianity in the Acts of the Apostles, and naturally dwells on and emphasizes the connecting link between his two histories, which was the distinct promise of the Holy Ghost: "And behold I send forth the promise of my Father upon you: but tarry ye in the city until ye be clothed with power from on high."—Luke xxiv. 49. "And being assembled together with them, he charged them not to depart from Jerusalem, but to wait for the promise of the Father, which, said he, ye heard from me: for John indeed baptized with water: but ye shall be baptized with the Holy Ghost not many days hence."—Acts i. 4, 5.

And it is worthy of notice how the exceeding importance of this promise was emphasized, not only by the declarations of Jesus to that effect, but also by an incidental illustration. For the disciples in their simplicity imagined that now their dreams of a temporal kingdom were to be realized, and put the thought in the form of a question before Him.

But Christ, in place of taking time to disabuse their minds of this expectation by entering into a lengthened description of the nature and object of His coming into the world, to live and die and rise again, simply drew their attention again to the great coming event, the gift of the Holy Ghost, intimating that He would guide them into all truth concerning these things. "But ye shall receive power, when the Holy Ghost is come upon you: and ye shall be my witnesses both in Jerusalem, and in all Judea and Samaria, and unto the uttermost parts of the earth."—Acts i. 8.

What a lesson for would-be teachers of the truths of revelation! Does it not admonish us to confine ourselves *chiefly* to showing men how to secure the gift of the Holy

Ghost, in the confident expectation that He, the Spirit of truth, would make plain to them all needful knowledge?

And further, what vast importance we are taught by this act of the Saviour to attach to this wonderful gift of God to us!

John, in his gospel, is more minute than Luke, in reproducing the words of the Master concerning the Holy Spirit, and because of their great import we quote them entire.

"He that believeth on me as the Scripture hath said, out of his belly shall flow rivers of living water. But this spake He of the Spirit, which they that believed on him were to receive: for the Spirit was not yet given."—John vii. 38, 39.

"And I will pray the Father, and he shall give you another Comforter, that he may be with you for ever, even the Spirit of truth: whom the world cannot receive; for it beholdeth him not, neither knoweth him: but ye know him; for he abideth with you, and shall be in you."—John xiv. 16.

"These things have I spoken unto you, while yet abiding with you. But the Comforter, even the Holy Spirit, whom the Father will send in my name, he shall teach you all things, and bring to your remembrance all that I said unto you."—John xiv. 25.

"But when the Comforter is come, whom I will send unto you from the Father, even the Spirit of truth, which proceedeth from the Father, he shall bear witness of me."—John xv. 26.

"Nevertheless I tell you the truth, it is expedient for you that I go away: for if I go not away, the Comforter will not come unto you: but if I go, I will send him unto you. And he, when he is come, will convict the world in respect of sin, and of righteousness, and of judgment: of sin, because they believe not on me: of righteousness, because I go to the Father, and ye behold me no more: of judgment, because the prince of this world is judged. I have yet many things to say unto you, but ye cannot bear them now. Howbeit, when he, the Spirit of truth, is come, he shall guide you into all truth: for He shall not speak from himself; but what things soever he shall hear, these shall he speak: and he shall declare unto you the things that are to come. He shall glorify me: for he shall take of mine and shall declare it unto you. All things, whatsoever the Father hath, are mine; therefore said I, that he taketh of mine and shall declare it unto you."—John xvi. 7.

From these passages it will be seen that the fact of the gift of the Holy Ghost, as a positive promise, to be realized in the near future, is established beyond doubt. And it is also evident from them, that when He should come it would be to remain to the end of time, in the same power and blessing of His first appearing. Further, this manifestation of the Blessed Spirit in believers was to be something entirely distinct from all former manifestations, and to be vastly more valuable. So much was this to be true, that in the comparison it might be truthfully said, that till the day of Pentecost the Holy Spirit was not given to the world, because Jesus was not yet glorified.

Again, whilst the Holy Ghost, in taking His place to preside over this dispensation, is described as both Empowerer and Comforter to believers, with equal, if not greater emphasis, He is promised to be their instructor and guide. For this office of Instructor or Guide is described with more minuteness than the others, as careful reading of the above passages will show.

But it is also seen in the fact that ever and anon Jesus, in His discourses with the disciples, leaves some things incomplete, intimating that when the Holy Spirit came He would fully supplement His sayings, and bring to their consciousness all He wished to say to them, even showing them things to come when needful.

Then, at different times, the Saviour seemed to be conscious that His words spoken to His disciples, were beyond their comprehension; but He contented Himself and them with the assurance that at the time of the advent of the Promise of the Father, they would, through the Spirit, fully comprehend them. "In that day ye shall know that I am in my Father, and ye in me, and I in you."—John xiv. 20. "And in that day ye shall ask me nothing."—John xvi. 23. As if saying that the gift of the Holy Ghost would meet all their desire to know concerning Him and the Father, and would so satisfy them concerning all things, that the sense of want would be obliterated.

But we also gather this important knowledge, viz.: That whatever of Divine guidance, under former dispensations, came to man, from the written oracles of God, or through His prophets, not excepting the Son of God, were, in the Spirit's dispensation, to come through Him, and Him alone. He, the Holy Ghost, is to guide believers into all truth, and He only. Not only

> "Apollo from his shrine
> Shall no more divine,
> With hollow shriek the steep
> of Delphos leaving,"

at the advent of the Spirit's rule, but even Moses is to vacate the law-giver's seat, and Christ Himself must leave the world for a little, to reappear in the person of the Holy Ghost, who is to speak only the words of Jesus, and be the direct and only channel of communication between man and God, until Christ shall come again to claim His own forever.

For if the Holy Spirit is constituted guide into *all* truth, where is the place for another guide? And where is the teaching of Christ, the last prophet, that gives authority for any additional guidance? Besides, where is the need of two-fold or multifold guidance, seeing the Guide Divine is omnipresent, and capable, with infinite ease, of individualizing Himself as companion and guest to every single follower of the Lord Jesus Christ?

CHAPTER VI.

THE PROMISE FULFILLED.

SUCH definite and positive promises demanded a speedy and exact fulfilment, else the very character of the promisor would be compromised.

Accordingly we have in the Acts of the Apostles a circumstantial history of all these promises fulfilled, and that fulfilment is so complete that no word of apology has ever been called for to excuse real or apparent defects.

Not only were the highly figurative predictions of the prophets fulfilled to the letter, but also the matter-of-fact descriptions of Christ were completely met. The description used by the Saviour Himself: "Pressed down and shaken together and running over," only faintly characterizing the gifts of God to man on and since Pentecost.

And this fulfilment of promises, to be complete, must not only take in their general aspects, but also their particular and minute details. Hence such statements as "He will guide you into *all* truth," "He will teach you all things. He will bring all things to your remembrance whatsoever I have said unto you." "He will take of mine and show it unto you." "He will show you things to come." "Be not anxious beforehand what ye shall speak: but whatsoever shall be given you in that hour, that speak ye: for it is not ye that speak, but the Holy Ghost,"—demand a minute fulfilment in the individual life of the believer.

And, moreover, these promises clearly embrace every individual child of God, or else they are confined to the twelve apostles. To admit them as spoken to Luke or Paul, in addition to the twelve, at once universalizes them in their application. But there is not the slightest hint at such limitation in the words of Jesus, and few if any since His day have undertaken to so curtail them.

Now, in support of our contention for the simple, natural meaning of these passages, we ask: Could any one wishing to teach the doctrine of Divine guidance, as applying to all individuals, for all things, and for all time, use stronger or more intelligible language to convey this meaning, than is used by Christ? Even place John's words, which express their fulfilment, beside them, and there is nothing in them either strained or extravagant:

"Ye have an unction from the Holy One, and ye know all things."—John ii. 20.

"But the anointing which ye have received of him abideth in you, and ye need not that any man teach you: but as the same anointing teacheth you of all things, and is truth and is no lie, and even as it hath taught you, ye shall abide in him."—John ii. 27.

Thus, according to John, the promises contained in the words of Christ were fulfilled to the letter, to all who, either on or after the day of Pentecost, received and retained the Divine gift. Was anything ever more distinctly promised or more minutely fulfilled according to the testimony of actual experience?

Nor are we left in a matter of such vast importance to the words of but one writer, for expressions which are freighted with the same general thought are scattered through all the writings of the New Testament. Peter intimates that the normal state of the Christian in this dispensation is, that even when he speaks, he does so as one led of the Spirit: "If any man speak let him speak as the oracles of God." And further, he adds: "If any man minister, let him do it as of the ability that God giveth."

Of course this might be made to refer to the general truth that all men, even infidels, receive whatever mental endowments they are possessed of which render them capable of ministering to the welfare of others from God.

But we incline to the belief that the apostle alludes here to that intimate union established between the child of God and the Holy Spirit, in this dispensation in which immediate, momentary guidance and ability for all emergencies were implied. But the practical recognition of the Holy Ghost in His intimate relation to Christians, as guide, has been so completely laid aside, that the argument drawn from this passage will be at once pronounced on by many as far-fetched.

Indeed, so strong will be this feeling in the minds of some readers, that common prudence would suggest the propriety of leaving out the passage, with the remarks upon it, altogether, lest the apparently inconclusive argument might tend to lessen the force of other quotations in this connection.

But we entreat the patient consideration of all to this further thought, to bring out which prominently has been the chief object of this quotation. During the times of the apostles, whilst the forgiveness of sins was made prominent in the preaching and teaching of all, still greater prominence was given to receiving the Holy Ghost in the Pentecostal sense, and most, if not all, teaching to believers recognized walking in the Spirit, that is, being guided by Him into all truth, as the great essential of holy living. Hence, where these were universally accepted truths, simple, and, to us, vague allusions to the doctrine of the guidance of the Spirit were understood, at that time, as containing in them the definite teachings of the whole subject.

Use this key, and see how readily the difficulties of Paul's letter to the Galatians, for example, are overcome. He boldly and pointedly proclaims that they were fallen from grace, because they had appointed unto themselves some *times* or *seasons* for special religious observance. That is, they had to an apparently small extent, ceased to walk in the Spirit and substituted the observance of rules and regulations for the one law of the kingdom of grace.

But so important did the great apostle consider this matter that he pronounced all who thus acted as already fallen from grace, and so serious did he consider the evil that like leaven he maintained it would speedily infect and destroy the whole church, unless promptly eradicated.

How utterly beyond the comprehension of the average Christian of to-day would be an epistle similar to this one, if addressed to one of our modern churches! Language which thus fairly unchristianized them for observing "days and months, and times and years," would be pronounced on as uncharitable in the extreme.

Or again, without this key to unlock the whole subject, how understand the most serious charge made against the Corinthians, accusing them of being carnal because one announced himself as having a preference for the teachings of Paul, another for those of Apollos and still another for those of Christ.

Surely there could be no serious fault here, nor is there when these things are not contrasted with the law of the Spirit. But it was just because such conduct indicated the rejection of the Holy Ghost as guide paramount into all truth, that Paul combats them with all his might. He was really defending the very citadel of the kingdom of Heaven. Nay, in his zeal he seems even to condemn the effort to obey the precepts of Christ, as laws, when they stood between the soul and the Holy Spirit as the one and only law of the spiritual realm.

From all of which we gain the distinct, positive knowledge, that the first teachers of Christianity so recognized the Holy Ghost as guide into all truth, as the Alpha and Omega of all practical knowledge of the will of God, that even apparently slight allusions to the subject can only be interpreted, or understood, by bearing in mind this fact.

And now it will be seen what a wealth of utterance, all going to establish the fact of the definite fulfilment of Christ's promises concerning the Comforter, may be found in the written word: "Received ye the Spirit by the works of the law or by the hearing of faith?" "Are ye so foolish? having begun in the Spirit, are ye now made perfect in the flesh?" now glows with light, and is so clear to the understanding that "he may run that readeth it."

And here we shall delay a little to quote a few of the many passages which give up readily their meaning when this law of interpretation is applied to them.

"But if any man hath not the spirit of Christ he is none of his," *i.e.*, hath not the Holy Ghost in Pentecostal sense as the law of life.

"And if Christ is in you the body is dead because of sin; but the Spirit is life because of righteousness."

"Christ in you," meaning the Holy Spirit as guide, or as the one and only law to the soul of the believer. This implies the giving up of all other laws, that is, their death because of failure or sin in their use. But the law of the Spirit secures *life*, because the outcome of obedient walk therein secures a righteous life.

"If the Spirit of him that raised up Jesus from the dead dwelleth in you, he that raised up Christ Jesus from the dead shall quicken also your mortal bodies through his Spirit that dwelleth in you." The Holy Spirit by the same power by which Christ was raised from the dead will enable you, in your own person, to do the whole will of God.

"But if by the Spirit ye mortify the deeds of the body ye shall live." If through obedience to the Spirit, as the only law of life, you turn alway from all other laws, as a means of holy living, you shall live, that is, succeed in living holy lives.

"For as many as are led by the Spirit of God, these

are sons of God." Those who, conscious of the presence of the Spirit, look to Him and to Him alone as guide into all truth, are the spiritual followers of Christ—"sons of God without rebuke."

"The Spirit also helpeth our infirmity: for we know not how to pray as we ought; but the Spirit himself maketh intercession for us." That is, in all our devotions unless they are begun, continued and ended in the Spirit, as our one and only guide in this thing, we of necessity walk in darkness.

"For the kingdom of God is not eating and drinking, but righteousness and peace and joy in the Holy Ghost." No outward expressions of a holy life, the result of following rules concerning eating, drinking, or any other outward acts, constitute the kingdom that Christ has set up in the world, but receiving and walking in the Holy Ghost, as the one and only rule of life, constitutes or secures to the believer the joy and peace of God and a righteous life before men—the true kingdom of God.

"That the offering up of the Gentiles might be made acceptable, being sanctified by the Holy Ghost." The Holy Ghost received in Pentecostal sense, by Paul's converts, as well as by those of Peter, the apostle to the Jews.

These few of the many such allusions the reader will recognize as taken, at random, from a part of Paul's letter to the Romans, and simply indicate the richness of the golden vein which runs all through the New Testament mine.

True it is that many of these and like nuggets of precious metal, unless assayed by the proper tests, are passed by as so many cobble-stones, and their richness is not discovered. But when brought into the Spirit's realm, and treated by His re-agents, especially when brought to the test of actual, personal experience, then they flame out in more than rainbow glories, displaying the resplendent brightness of the glory that excelleth.

But whilst the promises of Christ concerning the practical benefit of the coming Comforter to man as guide and teacher are alluded to in all parts of the epistles as fulfilled, and that too with sufficient distinctness to settle every doubt in the inquiring mind, we have, in the writings of Luke, incidental illustrations which speak, if possible, still more clearly and convincingly on this subject.

Take, for example, the history of the conversion of the Ethiopian eunuch. Need we trace Philip's steps, in this matter, how he received notification from the Spirit to go to a certain place, then was informed of the reason when the chariot containing the Egyptian prince passed along, his definite instructions to introduce himself, and the results of his obedience? Doubtless they are all familiar to the reader. But now, side by side, with all the details of this history, put Christ's distinct description of the work of the Holy Ghost with every individual follower of His who would receive the Spirit to be led by Him, and see if they do not dovetail into one another with a beauty of finish that should excite the admiration of all at the completed work of God.

Or even compare it with the Keilah incident, in the life of David, and who would sigh for the days of the prophets, and the ark of the Lord? that is, provided we accept the evident teaching of the Scriptures, that Philip in this narrative is simply a representative of all believers, and not restricted as an example of a small class of specially privileged favorites.

Then take the incident of the sudden call of Barnabas and Saul for a missionary tour: "And as they ministered to the Lord, and fasted, the Holy Ghost said, Separate me Barnabas and Saul for the work whereunto I have called them."

Evidently this call, received by these two apostles, did not startle the other disciples when they were informed of it; they simply verified it each for himself by the Holy Ghost who was given to all alike. Hence, with a unanimity, which is not only charming, but also a pled e of the success of the expedition, they set them apart for the work indicated.

The beauty of the picture consists in the simple, childlike faith in the literal words of Christ concerning the work of the Holy Spirit, and the action of all harmonizes with this literal interpretation of the promises of Jesus, and, as might be expected, the outcome of the expedition, thus inaugurated, was most satisfactory.

But again, Paul with Silas as a companion is on an evangelistic tour, not commenced, it is true, with the same formal sanction of the Spirit, but all the same under His immediate supervision. This is shown by the fact that there were distinct interpositions on His part to prevent them going to waste their energies in Asia or Bythinia, and to guide them to the exact points where they could accomplish the most for the Master. So, whether it was by a distinct voice heard in the centre of their being, by a vision of the night, or by the apparent deductions of a reasoning process, in all their movements they consciously verified that the promise of Christ, "He shall guide you into all truth," was no mere sentiment to them, but was a substantial promise which they proved for themselves, in all the acts of life.

And moreover it is evident that when they, the early teachers of the truth, spoke of receiving the Holy Ghost and walking in Him, they always included this practical thought of guidance through Him as the one and only law of life. And so generally was this understood, that they necessarily did not feel called on to be constantly emphasizing the fact. The Holy Ghost had not yet been robbed of His personal identity in the churches, or emasculated down to a mere influence, or His work in the human soul confined to simply witnessing to sins forgiven, and testifying to the divine origin of spiritual blessing, as is the case in the present day. Hence there was, obviously, no cause for discriminating against this modern teaching, seeing it had not yet appeared.

True, the *mystery of iniquity* had already begun to work, as is indicated in the letter to the Galatians—the little leaven had begun to permeate the whole lump. But that leavening process, which has in these days infected the whole church, was not then sufficiently pronounced to be noticed in all the writings on the subject of the gift of the Holy Ghost.

Hence when Peter, on the day of Pentecost, promised the Holy Ghost to all believers, he did not find it needful to explain minutely concerning the office of the Spirit, as described by Christ, but evidently implied that—in receiving Him—Christ's minute descriptions would be fulfilled to the letter in their lives.

Again, when Paul met the twelve Ephesian disciples and was the means of their receiving the Pentecostal gift, we find him leaving them in the hands of the blessed Spirit as if He, the Spirit of truth, would guide them into all truth. As if to obtain and retain the Heavenly visitant was to retain and show forth in the life the highest ideals conceived concerning the possibilities of grace.

And so we conclude this chapter concerning the promise fulfilled, as if a guide had conducted the traveller to some proud eminence, and after directing attention to a few of the prominent features of the magnificent landscape, as point after point in their progress was reached, he now leaves him with the whole sublime panorama before him to observe and muse at his leisure.

Behold the promise of Jesus fulfilled, not only as one magnificent whole, but in each minute detail, with unerring exactness!

CHAPTER VII.

THE TRUE ARGUMENT.

WE take our strongly intrenched position that the Bible alone can establish or disprove the doctrine of the Holy Spirit as guide into all truth.

Now, whilst having traversed but part of the ground, sufficient has been gone over to put it beyond question that the doctrine is taught clearly and emphatically in the sacred Scriptures.

Nevertheless, we would suggest that it is foolish in the extreme for any sincere lover of truth to leave this part of the subject with the least trace of doubt in the mind. If there be a residuum of doubt, the subject is of such practical importance that by all means it should be again traversed and further investigations made, till the assurance becomes complete that Christ promised, without limitation, that the Holy Spirit would guide the willing believer consciously into all truth, and that the early disciples so understood Him, and illustrated this their belief both in their writings and their lives.

Further, we maintain that the practice and belief of more modern Christians cannot be successfully contrasted with the early disciples, as an argument, to weaken the force of either Christ's words or the preaching or teaching of these first witnesses to the truth. If there be shown to be any discrepancy between them, it simply and only tells of modern Christians coming short of their full Pentecostal privileges. But it is the part of true wisdom to be so possessed with the strength of the Scriptural arguments establishing the fact of the guidance of the Spirit as a *vital* part of the system of Christianity, as to defy all efforts of reasonings many, or even apparent difficulties in the way, to weaken their force.

Furthermore, it must be accepted as a truth, revealed from God to man, and in no other way can it be received. But the Christ who promised it spoke the mind of God with authority, and established that authority by rising from the dead. If Christ then was and is the true revelation of God to man, then the possible guidance of every man into all truth by the Holy Ghost, who is given unto him, is a part of that revelation, and, therefore, like the mysteries of the atonement, or the apparently impossible fact of a general resurrection, it stands or falls on the divinity of Christ, and on that alone.

And be it well understood, that in this discussion, whenever we refer to the guidance of the Spirit, we mean *conscious* knowledge of the fact, on the part of the one so guided.

It would scarcely be in keeping with the dignity of the man Christ Jesus, to suppose that in all His minute promises concerning the offices of the Spirit, He was simply referring to the general superintendence of God over the world and His creature man. This truth was, before His coming, sufficiently clear to the heart of humanity. It was already the theme of the poet's song and of the prophet's teaching in the Israelitish nation, and had been from the beginning. Hence there would be no significance or value whatever in any promises concerning this thing that did not imply the conscious, unmistakable presence of a Divine guide who would make Himself known to the recipient of His favor.

This clear and positive statement is not only the inevitable inference from all Christ's utterances on the subject, but is amply borne out in incidental illustrations in the lives of the early disciples. When it is narrated that the Holy Ghost said, "Separate me Barnabas and Saul for the work whereunto I have appointed them," is there any room for imagining that they, the disciples, were not sure as to the person speaking to them? Who can add clearness to the statement that when Paul essayed to go to Asia, or to Bithynia, the *Spirit* suffered him not? How did Philip *know* that the Spirit told him to join himself to the Egyptian eunuch? We would feel like apologizing to the reader for taking so much time to establish what ought to be accepted as self-evident, were it not that the persistent efforts of modern writers and teachers have tended, almost universally, to throw doubts on the whole subject of *conscious* guidance by a recognized person as being really meant by Christ and the apostles when speaking of the Spirit's work.

But we declare it as our positive belief, that unless this common-sense thought be connected with the whole subject of Divine guidance, the doctrine of the Holy Spirit as guide into all truth becomes a delusion and a snare, and time spent on its investigation is worse than wasted.

And manifestly, if conscious Divine guidance is not guaranteed by the Gospel, then the fact should be stated in clear-cut sentences which would unmistakably bring out this testimony. It is a serious matter at this point to deal in vague, meaningless expressions. Christ either promised that his followers might accept the Holy Spirit as a personal guide into all truth, revealing Himself to their consciousness in so doing, or He did not. If He did not, but only emphasized the truth, already revealed to men, of God's general superintendence of the world, then the whole subject ceases to be of practical importance. For what practical difference does it make to me to be informed that the third person in the Trinity has now exclusive charge of the general and particular providences of life? It can, in the nature of the case, only appeal to my curiosity.

But the case is entirely different if I am informed that the third person in the Trinity has condescended to make Himself known to me as teacher and guide, giving me unmistakable evidence of His continued presence by becoming to me the one and only law of my life, so that with comparative ease I may prove at all times and in all places what is that good and acceptable and perfect will of God.

Whilst the first mentioned generalized truth would be no additional revelation whatever, the latter must command my attention, as promising practical benefits beyond expression.

Now, granting that the promises of Christ concerning guidance have reference to *conscious* guidance into truth, then it is further evident that unless that guidance comprehends all truth, it is still a valueless doctrine. For the very quality that gives intrinsic value to Divine guidance is the certainty of knowing that we are taking the right course in being so guided. If then it can be shown that only in some things has the Spirit undertaken to guide believers, then it follows that unless clear, unmistakable rules are furnished us, showing, without doubt, when and concerning what things He proposes to guide us into truth, we could never be certain of His guidance in anything, for there would ever be in the soul the fear that—concerning the matter in hand—it was not included amongst those things in which guidance Divine might be obtained.

Now, as a matter of fact, these clear, unmistakable rules are not given in the Bible—no, nor even hinted at. So it follows that positive Divine guidance must be provided for every moment of life, or, in the nature of the case, there can be no such guidance whatsoever.

We shall therefore proceed with what further investigations the subject demands, on the assumption that it is clearly established that the doctrine of conscious, Divine guidance by the Holy Spirit, for every believer, stands or falls with the divinity of the Lord Jesus Christ; that whatever may be the difficulties surrounding the subject, and however those difficulties may be enhanced by the misunderstandings and errors of those who have studied the subject, or professed to illustrate it in their lives, still the fact remains unaffected; they no more destroy its existence than clouds succeed in blotting out the orb of day.

CHAPTER VIII.

WHAT IS DIVINE GUIDANCE?

IT is now in order to examine into the nature of the subject itself, that is, to answer the question that characterizes this chapter; and it will now be better understood why we have delayed to this stage of the argument to so investigate it.

The quaint Isaak Walton emphasized a truth, too often ignored, when he insisted on it that the first step in the art of cooking one of his finny friends of the running brook was to catch the fish, and the application of this sage remark is obvious here. It were a strange proceeding to commence to discourse about the doctrine of Divine guidance, its nature and its modes of operation, whilst the slightest uncertainty remained concerning its existence. But now that we know of its certain existence, the question as to what we shall do with it is both interesting in the extreme and far reaching in its practical consequences.

"What shall I do with Jesus which is called Christ?" might well disturb the easy-going, voluptuous Pilate, for he could not ignore the patent fact that He was on his hands to be disposed of one way or another—there was no possible middle course. So with us this wonderful subject, which takes us as individuals in the circle of its mighty orbit, demands of us an answer to the question,

What shall we do with the doctrine of Divine guidance? and plainly intimates that our answer, in its practical form, links itself with our eternal interests.

But the answer which the former chapters indicate will reply to the question with sufficient clearness for the present stage of our researches, viz., It is some intimation to our consciousness by the Holy Spirit whereby we know that we are taking that course in all things, from moment to moment, which is the best possible under the circumstances, and which is therefore pleasing to God, and satisfactory to ourselves. Less than this could not be Divine guidance, more than this can hardly be desired.

When Scripture promises to man the forgiveness of all his past sins and iniquities it appeals to a conscious sense of want in man, and one of the proofs to the forgiven sinner that the act of grace emanates from the Divine heart is the fact that that sense of need is absolutely met.

So, too, in its appeals to the fear of death and future retribution, it discourses concerning *facts* in the soul's consciousness, and when they are, according to promise, taken away from the child of God, the sense of completeness in the work done speaks eloquently of the presence and power of God.

So, when the Bible promises guidance into all truth, it appeals to a felt want in the life of every believer.

> "Guide me, O Thou great Jehovah,
>   Pilgrim through this foreign land;
> I am weak, but Thou art mighty,
>   Lead me by Thy powerful hand,"

voices the aspirations of every sincere servant of the Lord Christ, and so, reasoning from analogy, this promise, to prove its Divine origin, ought, when fulfilled, to satisfy every legitimate longing of the soul of the Christian in this direction. And until that consummation, most devoutly wished by all, is realized, it ought not to be admitted that the promise is fulfilled in any individual case.

Gospel measure, indeed, is always on the line of "exceedingly abundant above all we ask or think," and so in this case also the abundant supply in guidance Divine should measure up to the sublime character and the exhaustless wealth of the bestower. "That we having all sufficiency in all things," "Who giveth to all liberally and upbraideth not," "If ye then being evil know how to give good gifts unto your children, how much more shall your Heavenly Father give!" "My God shall supply all your need according to His riches."

Such are samples of beneficence when it is measured out from His own resources by God Himself. Hence it is right to expect that when the full measure of God's idea concerning the promise of guidance is reached in human experience, there should not only be no lack to apologize for, or explain away, but language should prove "all too poor" to express the sense of satisfaction concerning the exceeding fulness of Gospel measure, whereby are done unto us exceeding abundantly above all we asked or thought.

Hence our contention here is that the experience in our lives of what is meant by the guidance of the Spirit should sweep away all our former ideals as far too low to measure up to its sublime fulness, and therefore, in place of finessing to bring the standard of our expectations down low enough to make it possible for God to reach them in our actual experience, we should the rather despair of having them high enough to meet the ability, yea, and pleasure of Him who illustrates in His acts the truth of His own law: "It is more blessed to give than to receive."

Then take the thought of doing all things so that life's record will be pleasing to God, and different passages of the Bible clearly imply the possibility of this desirable experience: "That you may walk worthy of God unto all pleasing," "That you may prove what is that good and acceptable and perfect will of God." Wesley has strung the thought of these and similar passages to his lyre in words familiar to many:

> "I want the witness, Lord,
> That all I do is right
> According to Thy will and word,
> Well pleasing in Thy sight."

Now if provision is made in the Gospel system whereby we may have the witness that our acts please God, when completed, is it any greater tax on thought or desire that we should know, even while the acts are being done, that His smile of approval rests upon us? But how have this approving smile unless we know we are doing the best possible under the circumstances? But this, however, is only another name for the guidance of the Spirit into all truth, and so even from the Scriptural starting-point of walking worthy of God unto all pleasing, we inevitably arrive at the doctrine of Divine guidance in its most pronounced form. And thus the deeper our researches the greater the number of arguments—all focussing in the one grand thought of conscious Divine guidance into all truth for all who accept the rich provisions of grace made and provided for them.

But, granted the correctness of the definition, how account for, or explain the manner of that conscious knowledge of the soul concerning the will Divine? How know that of a certainty the Holy Spirit communicates to our inner consciousness concerning His mind and will?

Now, before undertaking to investigate this part of the subject, we call attention to the fact, that it must be conceded to be of secondary importance. The great and important fact is that He, the Holy One, does undertake to make known to us continually the mind of God concerning being and doing according to His good pleasure. This being admitted, it rather belongs to the domain of curiosity to learn as to the manner of the operations of the Spirit. The employé who engages to serve his employer faithfully rightly feels that he has carried out his part of the contract when he has performed his allotted tasks, after being fully assured of the mind of his employer concerning them. To him it is, comparatively speaking, immaterial as to whether he learns of his duties by letter, by telegraph, by telephone or by word of mouth. The manner of communication to him is the master's business, and if he fails to learn his mind through no lack of attention on his own part, then, clearly, he cannot be blamed for failure to carry out the master's wishes.

So in this case. If the Holy Spirit has undertaken to

be to the believer his sole law in his life's work, then absolute willingness to obey Him, when he clearly, unmistakably understands His directions, fulfils all righteousness, even if there should be any failure on the part of his Guide to make him know the will of God concerning him.

These two propositions certainly go hand-in-hand. If the one be granted, the other must be admitted, and indeed, like a good rule, they will work both ways. For if the Holy Spirit as guide cannot clearly and unmistakably bring to the consciousness of the child of God the knowledge of His will under all circumstances, then manifestly He cannot guide him into all truth.

But, having arrived thus far in our investigations, it is evident, that the most sensible course to pursue, in continuing them, is to commit ourselves to the practice of the knowledge thus gained. For if it is perfectly clear to the mind that Scripture sets forth the Blessed Spirit as the guide paramount to the Christian, and if it is certain that He can make known the will of God to the soul of the believer continually, and if, further, our responsibility concerning guidance absolutely ends when we present the attitude of honest purpose and willingness to do the will of God at all costs, so soon as it is known, then it is evident that nothing is more in accordance with the dictates of reason, common sense and the Bible, or with our welfare both for time and eternity, than to gladly abandon ourselves without reserve to the Holy Spirit, and commence to be led by Him from this moment on into all truth.

But whilst this course appeals to our reason as the

true course of action, and is the speediest way to the solution of all imagined difficulties connected with the subject, yet, being the way of faith, it appeals so to our fears that hesitation, more or less prolonged, has characterized every seeker after truth, no matter how sincere or earnest in his quest. We

> " Linger, shivering on the brink,
> And fear to launch away."

But it is an encouraging thought that to us lingering hesitating ones, even when giving undue prominence to our fears, the golden gate into this rich banqueting house of the kingdom of grace still remains unclosed, and, after prolonged delay on our part, still woos us by its open portals to enter in to our own delight and the glory of its founder. For, "if any of you lacketh wisdom, let him ask of God who giveth to all liberally and *upbraideth* not."

CHAPTER IX.

THE MANNER OF DIVINE GUIDANCE.

NOW whilst it is true that the methods which the Holy Spirit may use in making known to us individually the will of God can only be known in the fact of such guidance, that is, by the actual experience of the fact, still there are many things which may be said in connection with this part of the subject whose tendency will be to clear away false views and presumed difficulties to the advantage of all concerned.

Strange and phantom-like notions prevail in the minds of many concerning the methods employed by God in making His will known to individual man in the earlier history of the race, and, unconsciously, these methods are accepted as necessary concomitants of such communications from God to man. And hence, insensibly, we arrive at the place where the phenomena attendant on the fact are exalted above the fact itself.

Take, for instance, the case of Abraham. God communicated to him His wish that he, Abraham, should leave Ur of the Chaldees and go to a land He would show him, and that in so doing He would greatly bless him in various ways. Now the simple fact that God communicated this knowledge to His servant, so that Abraham knew, of a certainty, the mind of God in the matter, will link it to every instance in the history of the world where a man was conscious of knowing the mind of God concerning any matter, however dissimilar the phenomena connected therewith.

Therefore, if a servant of God to-day learns with certainty that it is the will of his Master that he, for instance, should go to Africa, or China, as His missionary, this his call to leave home and friends and go to a foreign land is exactly similar in all essentials to the call of Abraham, provided, of course, that the call, in the latter case, is distinctly and directly from God, and is not the outcome of a reasoning process.

Certainly the attendant circumstances may exalt in importance the one far above the other. But granted the fact of direct communication from God to the consciousness of both, and there is no essential difference between them, as to the doctrine of Divine guidance.

And if the subject is looked at with sufficient care, it will be seen that the element of certainty is but little affected by outward phenomena. It is the inward persuasion, the conscious knowledge, that gives steadiness to action and is the real bed-rock of faith.

Imagine Abraham letting his whole career in life be swayed by any mere visible tokens of the Divine call, and see what room there would be for a vacillating faith. Suppose he could tell his friends of hearing an audible voice speaking to him from the Heavens, or of a wonderful vision by day or by night, or even of an angel or angels appearing to him with the commission, there would not be wanting some Eliphaz the Temanite, or Bildad the Shuhite, or Zophar the Naamathite, who, with well-rounded sentences, would prove to him the possibility of accounting for these phenomena as the outcome of undue mental strain, or physical disorganization, or the result of a mind slightly deranged through the fact of ancestors given to psychological pursuits, and that, therefore, it would be contrary to every dictate of reason and common sense to stake the fortunes of a lifetime on the bare possibility of these apparent visions not being pure hallucinations.

We readily grant that any or all these extraordinary accompaniments might in kindness be used and are frequently employed by God for arresting attention and strengthening faith. But we maintain that faith that is built on anything other than the conscious knowledge of God's will, as imparted by God Himself, rests on a precarious foundation; and we suggest that, in place of extravagant importance being attached to strange phenomena, the tendency should rather be to discount them in this connection; a thought which Jesus seemed to have in His mind when he remarked to the doubting Thomas, "Blessed are they that have not seen, and yet have believed."

Then, in this connection, closely scan the fact of the witness of the Spirit in the history of every truly converted child of God, and it will be seen that in every genuine instance the ground of confidence is real, heartfelt knowledge of the fact of such witness. True it is that there is endless variety in the accompaniments and surrounding circumstances of this Divine persuasion, but at best these are regarded as the casket which contains the jewel; and it is at once recognized by all as a sign of the spurious nature of the work done, or of some weakness in the individual, when there is evinced a tendency to exalt in the estimation the casket above the jewel it contains.

And so the real value of Christian testimony consists in conscious knowledge of sins forgiven, through the witness of the Spirit received into the inner consciousness of the soul so forgiven. The narrations of the circumstances, or even phenomena, attendant on this wondrous fact may be, and frequently are, of thrilling interest, and their very variety in the cases of different individuals gives a pleasing charm where numbers give their spiritual history. But they all take their significance from the glorious fact they enshrine—God making known to individual man His mind by direct, distinct communication.

Now, just as in the witness of the Spirit to the soul of man concerning sins forgiven, the great central fact is the witness itself, whilst all the circumstances surrounding that fact, although interesting, are of secondary importance,—so in the case of all communications to the soul by the Holy Spirit, as guide into all truth, the great central fact is the *consciousness* of knowing the will of God through the Spirit, whilst all the methods He adopts, or the variety of circumstances surrounding it, are of vastly inferior value. These all may be the casket, and may be, in their richness and volume, worthy of what they contain; but the enclosed gem is the "pearl of great price" which will repay every one who sacrifices all he has to obtain it.

Therefore it follows, that so long as the fact of *Divine* guidance exists, its value is neither enhanced nor diminished by its surroundings, whether these be of the nature of dreams, visions, voices, impressions, reasoning processes, intuitions, providences, human helps or Scripture passages.

CHAPTER X.

THE MANNER OF DIVINE GUIDANCE CONTINUED.

AS without faith it is impossible to please God in our attitude to Him in all things, so in this matter of guidance perfect faith in God the Holy Ghost is absolutely necessary that we may be led of Him into all truth.

But faith in Him includes in itself the absolute abandonment of our whole being to Him, that He may be able to utilize every avenue of approach to our consciousness for His purposes, and control every power and quality which goes to make up our being.

And the result of this complete surrender to God is the mystery hid in the ages, but which is now revealed, viz., God in the person of the Holy Ghost becoming identified with every part of our being as "Christ in us, the hope of glory," until the strange, anomalous state exists where it may be said to be—I and yet not I; or to use apostolic language, "I labored more abundantly than they all, yet not I, but the grace of God which was with me;" or the still more emphatic words of Christ, "It is not ye that speak, but the Spirit of your Father that dwelleth in you."

Now one of the abounding errors in the history of this doctrine is the persistent effort on the part of many to confine the operations of the Spirit to a limited part of the domain of human powers. Hence some make impressional guidance synonymous with Divine guidance. Others will add, to this limited part of our susceptibilities, visions and dreams, and other strange or startling phenomena, but confine His operations, in their creed, to these narrow bounds. Still others, with rigid law and stubborn will, limit His powers of impact upon the human soul to the simple channel of Scripture language.

But it is evident that all these limitations are the sure sign of that unbelief whose existence in the heart absolutely prevents full-orbed guidance by the Spirit. For it is manifest that, in dealing with us, the Holy Spirit must act upon us as intelligent beings to whom has been entrusted the royal quality of untrammeled free-agency. Hence all His operations must be in harmony with this our nature, and therefore are absolutely limited by our freedom of choice. He only then can, in the nature of the case, guide us to the extent of our perfect willingness to be so guided.

Now perfect willingness on our part must of necessity be the outcome of confidence in the Spirit's character and ability, that is, it is synonymous with faith, so that in vain that man looks for Divine guidance in his life who does not abandon himself with all his powers to the Spirit, that He, the Guide Divine, may utilize all these powers for His work of making him acquainted with the perfect will of God as it concerns him.

Hence it follows that the man who is really guided into all truth by the Holy Ghost is as certainly so led when apparently following the simple intuitions of his being, as when acted on by intense reasoning, or the rarer phenomena which occasionally, comet-like, rush into his being.

As above mentioned, many have exalted the strange phenomena known as impressions into the place of the peculiar work of the Holy Spirit, and the error has been with ease perpetuated because of the superstitious awe with which the phenomenon has been and still is regarded by even some great and good men.

The confusion which has existed and still exists around this section of the question will be better understood by reproducing an incident in the life of the late Dr. Bangs.

When a young man he was appointed to a circuit in the Western Peninsula of Ontario, and on one occasion, whilst passing, on horseback, one of the log cabins of the early settlers, a deep impression came to him that he ought to go into that house and make a pastoral visit, but the deep snow around the building and other difficulties inclined him to pass along without calling. As he went further away, however, from the spot, this strange impression deepened more and more, and became so strong, that, after riding upwards of a mile beyond, he actually turned back, went to the cabin and—found it empty !

Now, strange as it may appear, not only other writers, but Dr. Bangs himself, used this simple incident to throw discredit on the whole doctrine of conscious Divine guidance. And yet, if looked at closely, it will be seen that its bearing on this doctrine is very slight indeed.

Impressions, like dreams, come alike to saint and sinner, and of themselves affect the subject in hand no more and no less than any other phenomena of mind or matter. To this day philosophy is at fault in striving to account for them, and can lay down no safe rules by which to regulate them. Still it is a puzzling fact that some impressions, when followed, secure advantages to the one so obeying their weird, semi-supernatural voice, whilst others leave the party so following them the sport of an illusion.

Now if Dr. Bangs had looked beyond the impression to the Guide Divine till he knew distinctly His mind in the matter, then the course he took would be an illustration of Divine guidance; but as there is no evidence to show that he did so, we can dismiss this and all similar incidents as having no real connection with the subject in hand.

He treated the impression after the ordinary way, and in this instance was made the dupe of an illusion.

Impressional guidance, we further remark, does not change its character when given pious names, and he who abandons himself to its gyrations will make a tortuous pathway through life—whether he goes by the name of infidel, spiritualist, or Christian.

But, whilst impressional guidance is neither scriptural nor rational, it does not follow that the Holy Spirit may not use impressions, like any other susceptibility of our being, in His work. Indeed we should expect Him, with unerring wisdom, to enable us to accept the good from this source, when practicable, and reject the evil, and thus prove the superiority of the Spirit-led follower of Christ in this respect to all others.

And the same reasoning applies to dreams, visions and

other extraordinary phenomena of our being. Should a dream arrest our special attention, in place of applying to it the rules of the sceptic, and striving thereby to banish it from the memory,—through the ever-present Counsellor Divine we learn if it is charged with any lesson for our benefit, and if not, it is at once relegated to the class of dreams or visions to be forgotten, and no matter how startling its character it speedily passes away.

Thus we further emphasize the teaching of Scripture, that he who would secure the full benefits of Divine guidance can come to the Holy One with no limitations, the outcome of presumed superior knowledge concerning visions, dreams or impressions, or any other phenomena of mind or matter; but must frankly and fully surrender every department of his being, as to an absolute sovereign, who must have right of way through every channel of that being: "For who knoweth the mind of God, or being His counsellor hath taught Him?"

This general truth reaches much further in its application than many imagine. For if the Holy Spirit, the co-equal of Father and Son, refuses to guide him into all truth who puts any limitations upon Him either as to prescribing or circumscribing, then it follows that confining Him in His operations even to the written word would be manifestly so doing. And hence it is evident that they who stipulate beforehand what place the Bible should occupy in this connection must, perforce, fail in obtaining the full direction promised by Christ and ready to be imparted by the Blessed Spirit.

That this axiomatic truth is not accepted by many

must be admitted, for abundant facts testify to it; nevertheless we hesitate not to say that it is absolutely necessary to accept it and that without reserve.

For any stipulations, even in this direction, imply lack of confidence in the Holy One, which is, as shown above, simply another name for want of faith. And unbelief always has and always will be an effectual bar against the Spirit's work. One of the great indictments against the unbelieving Israelites, who perished in the wilderness, was that they "*limited the Holy One.*"

But, whilst not permitted to so limit Him, it does not follow that He will not use freely the sacred Scriptures in His work of guidance, or that He will put an embargo upon our Bibles and constitute them forbidden fruit, or place cherubim, with flaming swords, to cut off all access to the *lively oracles.*

To hold such thoughts concerning Him would make impossible that loving confidence in Him which is necessary for faith's foundation.

But whilst on the one hand He must have limitless control, even refusing to be hampered by our notions of Scripture utterance, on the other hand, He needs not the assistance of human device to aid Him in reaching our inner consciousness, such, for example, as opening suddenly the Bible, and noting the passage that first catches the eye, placing the finger, with averted face, on some one verse, and then noting its contents, and so assuming that the Holy Spirit guides the eye or the finger as to secure the knowledge needed for the present emergency.

It is true that the Holy Spirit demands right of way here also, and may not be questioned as to His right to require or permit us to pursue just such a course at times to learn the will of God concerning any matter. But he who adopts this method, as a rule, or would confine the work of the Spirit to guiding the muscles of the hand or the eye so as to secure suitable passages, is in extreme danger of making a mere fetish of his Bible, and will most assuredly fail in his quest after guidance into *all* truth.

The same line of argument will at once show that, whilst we may not oppose our *reason* as a bar to the Spirit's work, without forfeiting all the benefits promised in connection with this subject, that, at the same time, He has full right to guide us through all the powers of the mind. And a conviction arrived at by a distinct reasoning process may be as clearly understood in the consciousness as the voice of God to the soul as if that conviction came to us through any other channel, no matter if purely miraculous in its character.

And the same may be said of common sense or intuitive knowledge. It matters not how or what methods are adopted, if we are led by the Spirit, evidently, we must reach the truth, or the Holy Spirit fails in His ability to make good the promises of Christ.

But the question is often asked, Does the Holy Spirit ever lead contrary to reason or the Bible? Now, whilst we hesitate not to reply that neither is possible, nevertheless He may require us to follow Him with reckless faith when He guides contrary to our notions of Bible teaching, or even of what is reasonable.

For if the Holy Spirit in His work on the human heart contradicted His work as Inspirer of the Bible, or even threw contempt on reason or intuition, the gifts of God, there would be rare confusion in the household of God, for it would illustrate Christ's description of a house divided against itself. It could not long stand. All this is so certain that it needs no demonstration.

But on the other hand, it is by no means certain that the one who looks for Divine guidance has the perfect mind of God concerning all Scripture, nor yet is capable of pronouncing on every operation of his mind as a part of an absolutely correct reasoning process. Therefore, to arraign the Holy Spirit at the bar of our reasonings or notions of Bible truth would be manifestly absurd, and necessarily prevent the possibility of *Divine* guidance.

Therefore in epitomizing the above thoughts and reasonings in a definite reply to the question asked, we maintain that the Holy Spirit guides into all truth, as an absolute sovereign, who brooks no limitations on the part of finite man to His benign sway; and whilst He always guides into truth which is in perfect harmony with the Scriptures, the inspired word of God, and with every emanation of God, as reason and intuition, nevertheless He is not amenable to the law of human reason or human notions of what is revealed truth. And further, He claims right of way throughout every part of our being, that all our powers of mind, body and estate may be utilized by Him in securing for us the fulfilment of all Christ's promises concerning guidance Divine.

CHAPTER XI.

THE EXTENT OF DIVINE GUIDANCE.

INCIDENTAL ILLUSTRATIONS.

WE have in more than one place already indicated our answer to this thought. But as the hottest contests are about this part of the subject, it will be necessary to be still more exhaustive in its treatment.

We have noticed that incidental illustrations awaken the dislike of many, and we presume the reason is that their tendency is to bring the subject out from mere generalized thought into practical workable shape.

This awakens the suspicion that generalized statement as far as practical results are concerned is like mimic warfare, a pleasing spectacle to all, and awakens no opposition from any, seeing it neither calls for real exposure to danger, on the one hand, or for definite results on the other.

One may indulge in fancy word-picturing concerning the glorious nature of guidance into all truth, and be as extreme and comprehensive as the Scriptures are in statement, provided he ends with a prayer for its attainment or an exhortation to secure its benefits. For in that prayer or exhortation the hearer detects the absence of any call to a real warfare, and is conscious that the whole subject can be dismissed with a pious aspiration unuttered or expressed.

Hence as our object is stern, uncompromising battle for the truth—truth not only to be accepted in its general aspects but to be utilized in every-day life by all lovers thereof—we shall not shrink from running the gauntlet of possible hostile criticism through utilizing incidental illustrations drawn from *personal* history; and we shall use personal references in this connection chiefly for the reason that we are best acquainted with such incidents, not only with the incidents themselves, but with all the motives and arguments accompanying them.

We are fully aware that this method of argument will leave us open to the suspicion of being swayed by unworthy motives. But the extreme value of the subject in hand and our intense desire that many others should become partakers of all the far-reaching advantages connected therewith, is our excuse for braving such criticism.

We have in a former chapter alluded to the subject of impressions. Once when stationed on a mission, the following incident occurred. We had left home to be absent several days. But on the morning of the first day of absence, a strong impression seized us that we should return home, as being particularly needed there. So strong was this impression that we felt it would shadow our footsteps continually if we went on with our intended work.

But the business in hand was urgent, and so we were in a puzzling dilemma. On the one hand was the possibility of being made the dupe of an illusion, at the cost too of serious neglect of needed work. On the other, was the possibly continued uneasiness from the apprehension of impending calamity. Now we maintain that the history of such incidents is that sometimes when the impression is followed the result is satisfactory, and sometimes not; and few persons there are who do not know this by experience.

True it is that the instances where benefit has been the result are the ones which are paraded both in print and conversation, whilst the others, probably a more numerous class, are consigned to oblivion, and so the whole subject of impressional guidance, like patent medicines, has been advertised on its occasional merits.

But the desire came to us at that time to see if there was not provision made in the gospel to settle this perturbing question, once and forever, by learning exactly what to do, so that whilst doing it we might know with absolute certainty that we were taking the right course.

We examined, in memory, for we had not as yet arisen from our couch, all Scriptures bearing on the subject, and finally settled on the promise contained in the first chapter of the epistle written by James.

"If any man lack wisdom." This we admitted was our case. We lacked the wisdom of knowing with certainty which course was the better to take. "Let him ask of God, who giveth to all liberally and upbraideth not." Thus encouraged we asked of God what course we should take, but still our hesitation was not gone. Manifestly then something more than formal asking was needful. "But let him ask in faith, not wavering." "For let not that man (who wavereth) think that he shall receive anything from the Lord." So clearly it was necessary to get a practical idea of what faith meant in this connection.

We shall not weary the reader with all the thoughts and reasonings of our mind at this point. Suffice it to say, that the result was that again we asked God for wisdom, with the understanding, on our part, that it would be given us freely, and that then in taking the course that seemed best we would be acting out God's wisdom in the matter, assuming that whatever might be the apparent, immediate results, we could and would positively believe our course then taken the very best, and that that confidence must last to the very judgment day.

Thus treated the impression deepened, and we returned home, not as led by our impression, but as led by the Holy Spirit, who, in this case, used an impression, according to His sovereign right, to make known to us His good pleasure.

The sequel of the story proved the urgent need of returning home at that time, indeed, our return home was of such conspicuous importance that the whole incident stands out in our life as calling for adoring gratitude for signal mercies received at the hand of the God of providence.

But although the incident itself is of thrilling interest to us, nevertheless, as an incident pure and simple it sinks into insignificance when compared with the valuable practical lesson concerning Divine guidance of which it was to us the exponent. For since then no lingering hesitation has characterized our life concerning the perplexing subject of impressions in connection with the doctrine of Divine guidance.

As a matter of history, many an impression since then has been flung aside as of no practical value, whilst others have been utilized by our Guide for important results.

Has not the reader often had soul-trouble concerning its inability to judge righteous judgment concerning men and acts? For example, conduct on the part of a professing Christian has been witnessed which plainly indicated the absence of the spirit of the Master. But after a short interval of time the same party has been heard to speak, either in Christian testimony, or in prayer, with great unction and power.

And now the unrest of soul begins. There may be the sincere desire to believe that this apparent unction is backed by a holy life, but the judgment sturdily refuses to yield to the importunate pleadings of the sympathies and pronounce on those actions as right, and so the result is perplexity and trouble of mind, ending often in loss of relish for the service of the Sanctuary, and not unfrequently in making shipwreck of faith and a good conscience.

Once, when enduring this perplexing trial, we resolved to have it settled once for all through the ministry of the Spirit, or know that there was no provision made for such emergencies in the Christian's life.

The party in prayer was had in reputation by all, was not only useful as a conspicuous official of the church, but in his private character commanded the respect of the whole community. But we had, unwittingly, witnessed in him a spirit of retaliation which we could not harmonize with the precepts of the Gospel of Christ, and so we were conscious that the old battle which had never been settled by more than an armed truce was recommenced.

The subject of our thoughts was engaged in zealous, unctuous prayer, and we were striving, with sincere desire, to believe that his life harmonized with his utterances. Our success in this direction not being complete, suddenly the thought came to us, Why not let the Holy Spirit guide you into the truth concerning this thing?

Again we put in practice the process of reasoning narrated in the foregoing incident, although for obvious reasons in a much shorter space of time, and the outcome of it all was that we came to the conclusion that there was some radical defect in this brother's Christian experience, so whilst he was praying for others there was an urgent call on us to pray for him, which accordingly we did. And so, for some weeks after, whenever he led in prayer, our sympathies were aroused in importunate prayer that he might discover his error and learn the more excellent way.

It was not long after that we had the satisfaction of hearing this brother publicly testify that the Holy Spirit had revealed to him the defects of his Christian experience, and that after an all-night struggle he had learned to put on Christ after the New Testament pattern.

And so we have found the doctrine of Divine guidance not only helpful, but absolutely settling, in such serious experiences of life where the demand is to judge righteous judgments concerning our fellow professed Christians.

And we have further learned by experience that righteous judgments in the Spirit, even when they are condemnatory in their character, are not used as a cloak of maliciousness, but by love are the means of enabling us to serve one another.

CHAPTER XII.

INCIDENTAL ILLUSTRATIONS CONTINUED.

LAST winter there came to live in a house opposite our residence a family consisting of father, mother, and several small children. Both parents were open sinners, being addicted to drink and the use of obscene language, so as to often foul the night air and prove a conspicuous nuisance to our part of the street. It was all the more noticeable, as Bleeker Street makes some claims to respectability, and they were the only family that did not accord with its character.

After a time the propriety of our making a pastoral visit to this habitation of open sin was forced upon us, not only by our own thoughts, but also by the admonition of others. But all we did at the time was to direct the attention of a policeman to the state of affairs over the way, requesting him to look after the parties during the late hours when the uproar generally commenced. Our reply to those who requested us to visit the family as a minister and professed follower of Christ was, that our time was not yet.

Now, here the practical question of great importance comes up, Was it possible for us to know with restful certainty that it was not proper for us to make a pastoral visit to that home at that time, with the admitted possibility of never so visiting it?

This question is generally treated after a snap-judgment sort of style, and, of course you should go, is universally the answer; whilst many a Scripture passage is quoted to enforce it, as, "To him that knoweth to do good and doeth it not, to him it is sin."

But our reply to this was, and is, that our action was not the outcome of a hastily formed judgment, but the result of many years of experience and close study of the whole far-reaching question involved in this one incident.

For, granted that of course it was our duty to visit these wicked parents, thus providentially brought to our door, why not of course visit other families near by, who, although not so openly wicked, were known to us as unforgiven sinners in the sight of God? Or, indeed, why not of course visit other families and find out their spiritual needs, seeing we have a right to suspect that the majority of all the families in the city are careless of their immortal interests?

Now it is evident that we could not visit all such, and so from absolute necessity there must be a discrimination on our part, a selection amongst many claimants for the time at our disposal for such visitations.

Then comes up the question, How are we to know the way to utilize our limited time for the best possible results in such an illimitable harvest-field? Shall we decide, in an off-hand way, that proximity and open sin should decide as to the first claims on our time? Well, such arguments look plausible, and could easily be fortified by apparent Bible sanction. But let them be adopted as a cast-iron rule, and to the thoughtful worker they will soon be seen to have serious defects.

But we wish it to be clearly understood that our quest has not been for some rule of practice, which was to be advertised on its occasional merits, whilst its more numerous demerits were to be ignored.

The question decided by us in refusing to visit this home at that time was, Is it possible for us to know with *certainty* the best thing to do with such an opportunity, and we took the ground when we decided not to go just then, leaving the whole matter concerning the future in uncertainty, that we took exactly the right course.

Moreover, we were perfectly prepared to stand the scrutiny of the judgment day concerning our decision in the case. When we drew the attention of the police to the street nuisance we knew that we had, for the present, done our whole duty in the matter, and so we went on with our life-work, untroubled by any spectred uncertainties visiting us during the times of prayer, or thoughts of future retribution.

Once it was not so in our life. More than once have we slowed up our horse, hoping that some pedestrian ahead of us would turn into some other road and thus not make it necessary for us to invite him into the buggy and talk to him about his spiritual welfare, seeing we shrank from such pastoral work at that time. We were trying to regulate our pastoral work then by a rule, and found our rule a hard taskmaster, and ourselves a bond slave to its inexorable demands.

Not that we can speak of uniform failure in carrying out this rule, for there is living to-day at least one Christian who was converted to God whilst sitting by our side in our buggy.

Indeed, as we look over our pastoral work, conducted after the usual method of set rules and plans, whilst the yoke of bondage ever and anon galled and chafed our neck, nevertheless, we can gratefully recall definite results connected with it beyond what is common.

We have had the satisfaction of rejoicing over sinners converted, not only in our buggy, but whilst riding on horseback by our side, whilst walking by the way, as well as at their own homes. There are those in heaven to-day whom we had the extreme pleasure of leading to Christ in doing pastoral work.

We make these personal allusions to show that, in discussing this practical question, we are not simply speculating, or hunting for some excuse for idleness in the Lord's vineyard, but as investigating concerning the very best way to utilize time in pastoral work.

If, for example, the season for pressing the claims of religion on this sinful couple was not opportune, would it not be a gain to us in other directions of Christian work that we should be saved from depressing rebuff and positive loss of time? Who that studies the nature of man but must confess that there are a hundred times in the year unfavorable to pressing the claims of religion to one favorable one, so that when one *chances* it, the chances are a hundred to one against his calling at the right time.

But can one with unerring certainty know that one-hundredth opportunity? Well, the question is worthy of a thoughtful consideration, and he who should treat it flippantly would not thereby necessarily establish his reputation as an anti-fanaticist.

Now we hesitate not to say that in the law of the Spirit this question is so satisfactorily answered, that to us the change from former laws to this one law of the Spirit is as from darkness to light—"the former dispensation to us hath no glory by reason of the glory which excelleth."

The sequel: Weeks went on, and still the drunken pair ever and anon indulged in their orgies, although—thanks to the police, we will presume—the midnight air was no longer polluted by their obscene epithets. But a day came when one of the children rushed into our house, saying their baby was dying. It was speedily found to be correct, for the child died in its mother's arms that afternoon. After a time the father came home drunk.

We then for the first time looked into that home of intemperance. What a scene we witnessed! The child lying dead in one room, the mother, sober, but with the marks of continued excess upon her person, whilst the home spoke loudly by its wretchedness of their sin.

Not that the building itself was an inferior one, for it was not, but it bore unmistakable evidence of being the home of drunkenness. The father was maudlin drunk, too disgusting a picture to truthfully describe. And yet he gave evidence of being beyond the ordinary in intelligence. Evidently he was an English gardener of extra skill and intelligence.

We stayed but a few moments at that time, but, next morning, with the same certainty that hitherto we refrained from making pastoral visits, we realized that our opportunity had come, and called upon them. We had lengthened conversation and prayer with them, and ere we left, both professed to be rejoicing Christians. And that it was not a mere profession was afterwards evidenced by a life of sobriety and attention to the outward claims of religion, including family worship. They have since moved to another part of the city, but we learn that theirs is still a reformed, Christian home.

Now, we freely confess that we do not parade this incident as if it shamed other workers in their pastoral labors, for we have no doubt but many Christian workers can point to many similar incidents as the result of their pastoral work.

What we do draw attention to in the relation of this incident is the fact, that whilst successful work was done for the Master, it was accomplished at the least possible expenditure of time and thought taken from other Christian work of equal, if not of greater, importance, whilst the relation of the incident entire helps, in our opinion, to emphasize our answer in the affirmative to the question, Can a Christian do the right thing at the right time in pastoral work, and *know* that he is so doing it?

Wishing to take the cars late one Saturday afternoon on an important mission, dictated by the Holy Spirit as clearly as was the call to Barnabas and Saul for similar work, we found we had scanty time for reaching the station before the cars would leave.

Two courses were open to us, either to go out of our way a distance, when, if the car on that street happened to be passing at the right moment it would enable us to catch the train, otherwise not; the other was to go on our way, but somewhat further, to meet another line of cars, when the same peradventure would meet us.

By faith we looked for Divine guidance, and with perfect confidence took the first mentioned course, and failed not to reach the depôt in time, for the car passed at the moment of our arrival at the street.

And similar instances could be given in abundance from ordinary every day life to illustrate the fact of the practical value of this gospel provision in life's activities.

Not that one who accepts guidance Divine in all the activities of life carries with him an insurance policy against the possibility of missing a train or meeting with apparent loss of time or any form of what is called loss or disappointment in life. For such a result might well be questioned as being really desirable or profitable

But what we do contend for is, that he who walks in the Spirit, in full-orbed guidance, has the abiding consciousness amidst all life's perplexing changes that he walks worthy of God unto all pleasing, and hence does not walk in the darkness of uncertainty concerning any matter however great or trivial. He knows by happy experience that the steps of the good man are all ordered by the Lord, that none of his steps do slide, and that no good thing is, from moment to moment, being withheld from him walking uprightly, *i. e.*, in the Holy Ghost.

Hence our contention is, both from the clear unmistakable teaching of Holy Writ and the ample corroboration of years of personal experience, that the work of the Holy Spirit as guide into all truth extends to every matter, whether great or small, that touches human life.

And what man, we ask, can sit in judgment on any matter and pronounce, with oracular certainty, as to whether it is great or small, or, for that matter, as to whether it is sacred or secular in its character ?

A friend of ours once delayed his journey to town a few moments to break some pine for kindling—a trivial matter an oracle would doubtless say—and yet it resulted in the loss of an eye, for a splinter struck the eye ball and resulted in that sad calamity.

By an oversight of a conductor we once took a certain car on a train—a trifling matter—but simple as it was it saved us from being precipitated over a high embankment in a car where several were killed.

At best we are but as blind men walking amongst pit-falls and snares, and every step is taken into possible disaster and ruin. Occasionally something of the true significance of passing events, in all their vast possibilities of good or evil, is revealed to us, and yet the suspicion will haunt us that possibly multitudes of others, which we still look on as of trivial importance, are freighted with infinite value, and may pour upon us their accumulated weight of weal or woe at some future date.

Hence, he is a most reckless thinker, who will admit the possible benefit to man from conscious Divine guidance in the so-called momentous incidents of life, but hesitates not to rule it out as unnecessary in matters of apparently trivial importance.

Besides he is not scriptural, for the Bible requires us in such trivial acts as eating and drinking to do all as to the Lord, and enjoins upon slaves, in performing the menial acts of their life of toil, to do all things heartily to the Lord. Whilst Christ taught that even in the things which appertain to clothing the body, all should be left to the regulation and care of God.

Nor would our oracle be any more fortunate in pronouncing on any act in life, as to whether it might be classed as sacred or secular. For by positive prediction it was taught that whatever line of demarcation existed, under the old covenant, to distinguish between what was holy and what was not, was to be obliterated in the Spirit's dispensation, until the very bells on the horses, and the pots in the homes should be called holy unto the Lord. And accordingly, as we have seen, even eating and drinking and menial acts of service are, in the New Testament, exalted to the dignity of religious services. What God hath cleansed let not even an apostle call common or unclean.

CHAPTER XIII.

THE DOCTRINE OF DIVINE GUIDANCE IN ITS SCOPE.

NOW whilst the doctrine of the guidance of the Spirit into all truth is not absolutely the baptism of the Holy Ghost, as witnessed on the day of Pentecost, nor the gift of the Holy Spirit as spoken of after that event, nevertheless, it is so identified with it, and constitutes so large a part of what is implied by walking in the Spirit, that the one always must, in correct scripture nomenclature, include the other, and hence these are almost interchangeable terms.

And, moreover, it will be discovered by any who regard the matter with sufficient care, that the fact of this doctrine being practically ignored accounts for the unsatisfied longings, so general amongst Christians, concerning Spiritual blessings. For how can the Holy Ghost come to the soul of man in Pentecostal fulness when man, through unbelief, denies to Him his full rights? In vain does any one undertake to bring the third person in the Trinity down to his limited measure or thought.

Again and again has He, as the promise of the Father, come to take up His abode with us, at our importunate call, but so soon as we hesitated to let Him have right of way, as guide into all truth, so soon was He, however grieved and reluctant, forced to depart, and leave us with unsatisfied longings, to mourn with unavailing regret the absence of Him who alone can satisfy.

And such has been the experience of multitudes of God's people. No matter if hesitancy to be led by Him, as the sole law of life in every direction has been because of honest fear of fanaticism, or of proving an injury, through failure, to the cause of God; no matter if the result of false notions imbibed through the teachings of great and good men, no matter if the result of our own reasonings concerning the subject, or of observing the vagaries of others, still the fact that under any plea the Holy Ghost is denied His proper place in the Christian's life as guide paramount into all truth, the result must be the same. The Holy One must, in justice to Himself, and loyalty to the truth, vacate His loved abode, and leave us the lawful prey of unfulfilled desires.

Whence those soul groanings in all our churches which fill and torment the air? voiced in such language as, O for more love! O for spiritual power! Send the Holy Ghost in Pentecostal power! O for a Pentecost! Or, slightly changed to suit the pulpit, What the church wants is more Holy Ghost power! And the pews throw it back with emphasis, What the pulpit of to-day needs is more of the power of the Holy Ghost.

"Does the ox low over its fodder?" the prophet significantly asks, implying that the cry of want indicates the absence of the thing desired.

And yet, as we before intimated, multitudes who join in that sad cry of want, for longer or shorter periods of time, have known that want satisfied. The newly regenerated soul, jubilant with the conscious witness of the Holy Ghost to sins forgiven, and adoption into the family of Heaven, does not help to swell that cry, nor yet the believer, who, whether under the name of a clean heart or the baptism of power, or any other of the modern substitutions for what the apostles called the gift of the Holy Ghost, has welcomed, for the first, or hundredth time, the Blessed Spirit into the heart; for the exceeding glory of His incoming always renders it impossible in the mean time, although that period be short in its duration.

But so persistent is unbelief in the power and willingness of the Holy Spirit to constitute Himself the one law of life, and so generally has this want of faith prevailed, that with the great mass of believers these bright spots in Christian experience are few and far between, and so the great mass of Christians go to swell the volume of that painful wail, until, like the voice of many waters, it fills all the air, and gives character to nearly all religious service. As if man, in his multiplied capacity, would rend the heavens, and force the Almighty to terms, and cause Him to change the law of faith into that of importunity.

But, in spite of all, God maintains His integrity of character, and still points to the words of an apostle as the necessary condition of that want being met once and for all time: "Received ye the Spirit by the works of the law or by the hearing of faith? are ye so foolish, having begun in the Spirit are ye made perfect in the flesh?"

The fundamental nature of this doctrine is witnessed

in that if it be fully accepted and acted out by faith, in life, the result must be, that, sooner or later, we will be led into all Pentecostal truth. And further, whilst being so led, it must secure for us the consciousness of being on the direct road to these truths.

So, we repeat it, to accept the Holy Ghost as guide, and give Him full right of way, that is, act out in life perfect faith in Him, is tantamount to securing all the experiences of the New Covenant made and provided for the present and every consecutive moment of our lives.

Napoleon Bonaparte, when he undertook to drive the British from Toulon, pointed to a certain fort of the enemy, and exclaimed, "That is Toulon," meaning that if that was captured the British must evacuate the city; and so he bent all his energies to secure the coveted position, and when success crowned his efforts, true to his prediction, the city was vacated, and his victorious army marched in and took possession.

So, in this case, we might point to the doctrine of Divine guidance as all that is implied in Pentecost, for, when lived out in life, all else is sure to be secured. But if left out of creed or practice, then it is impossible to come into permanent possession of our full heritage of New Covenant blessings.

Therefore it will be seen that our theme, although at first promising to be short and restricted in its application, necessarily takes in for consideration Pentecost, with all that is implied by the gift of the Holy Ghost on that day of power and blessing.

The Promise of the Father was confined in its final

bestowment to the six score personal followers of Jesus—those who had accepted Him as the true Messiah, and were obedient to His words. The test of faithful obedience was in that they remained, in strict compliance with His commands, at Jerusalem, waiting for this wonderful gift, concerning which Jesus had discoursed so much.

It is reasonable to presume that this one hundred and twenty persons were all or nearly all of the many who had listened to the teachings of Jesus who had sufficient faith in Him to tarry in the city for the promised boon. No doubt more would have been partakers of like blessing had they evinced like faith in Christ.

These few score souls were a glad, triumphant company, for Luke tells us that they were together as one: "These all with one accord continued steadfastly in prayer;" and elsewhere the same writer describes them as "returning to Jerusalem with great joy, and were continually in the temple blessing God." Hence we maintain that it was from no defect in their religious character, as compared with the saints of former dispensations, that they were required to wait for additional spiritual blessing. What they were to receive was something over and above all the possibilities of spiritual blessing under former dispensations of grace.

Hence those writers who point to crises in the lives of Isaiah, Jeremiah and other Old Testament worthies, as similar to the blessing received by these happy, united Christians, only confuse matters, for the Holy Ghost, the distinguishing gift of this dispensation, was only known then as a prophecy of some good thing to come.

Manifestly there can be no comparison in the case, and therefore all efforts in that direction must of necessity be misleading.

We repeat, that little company in the upper room represented the best saintship under the Old Covenant, and hence they were not seeking the blessing of holiness, as represented in the life of any or all former saints, seeing they represented amongst their number the best possible saintship of that age. They were waiting for what

> "Prophet and priest desired to see,
> But died without the sight."

That which was to be so superior in every respect to all former spiritual experiences, that, to use the language of Paul, "the former would have no glory by reason of the glory that excelleth."

This ten days' delay was evidently of Divine appointment, for no reason is given by either Jesus or any of His immediate followers. Nor do the necessities of the case show any cause for protracted waiting, for as the above quotations show, every sign of preparation that the human mind could demand was witnessed as certainly on the first day as on the tenth.

But, further, it is evident that this waiting experience was to be unique in the history of the Church, and its repetition never to be called for. For when once the Holy Ghost, sent of the Father at the instance of the Son, should come, He was to abide forever, and all who in the future should receive Him would do so by faith, that is, in their case, by simple, glad acceptance, and every consecutive moment after Pentecost was to be freighted with that grand possibility.

And now at length their obedient faith was fully rewarded, for, on the tenth day after our Lord's ascension, the promise of the Father, He who had been so minutely described by Christ, came to their prepared hearts to abide with them continually as their empowerer, joy-giver, teacher and guide.

As the former dispensation had been ushered in with signs and wonders, to impress the mind of man with its Divine origin, so in this case they were not wanting, and for a like purpose. Hence the sound of a mighty, rushing wind, the cloven tongues, as of fire, and the gift of tongues. But these, like the phenomena witnessed at the giving of the Ten Commandments at Mount Sinai, were necessarily temporary in their character, and had no promise of Christ which guaranteed permanency to them. But the gift of the Holy Ghost, then for the first time definitely received into the heart and life of the believer, had been promised as the permanent characteristic of this last dispensation.

For they were all filled with the Holy Ghost, and remained so filled, and Peter, to the multitude of persistent seekers, who, on the same day desired help, was authorized to promise the same fulness of Gospel blessing. His words are: "Repent ye and be baptized, every one of you, in the name of Jesus Christ unto the remission of your sins; and ye shall receive the gift of the Holy Ghost. For to you is the promise, and to your children and to all that are afar off."

Again, when some of the apostles were arraigned before the rulers, it is said: "Then Peter, *filled* with the Holy Ghost, said unto them." Again, it is narrated, in the fifth chapter, how the disciples after having been brought before the leading officials of the Jewish nation, and roughly treated, and commanded to desist from preaching Christ, that when gathered together praying, "the place was shaken wherein they were gathered together; and they were all filled with the Holy Ghost, and they spake the word of God with boldness."

It is true that much effort has been put forth to make this incident an apology for the conspicuous absence of the Pentecostal gift from modern experiences, by maintaining that this fact proves that the baptism of the day of Pentecost was a simple, temporary blessing, ephemeral in its nature, and corresponds to those times of emotional refreshment which occasionally characterize religious gatherings; implying if not actually asserting that the gift was an influence and therefore could be measured out in smaller or greater quantities, or was subject to comparison. For, say they, it was evident the intensity of the baptism received on the day of Pentecost had somewhat lessened, and so it was needful that they should be rebaptized or refilled with the Spirit.

This view of the case would also bring down the doctrine of Divine guidance into the same narrow dimensions, and in place of a personal Guide, ever present, with all the attributes of the Godhead, Divine guidance would be an occasional influence or afflatus, subject to all the uncertainties which time, place and surrounding circumstances could throw into it.

Now, in combating this view, it is evident that it should not be met in the spirit of debate, that spirit which tries, for the sake of mere argument or to make good one's assumed position, to establish the falsity of an opponent's contention. It should be examined into for the truth's sake, and with the real purpose of adopting this view of the case if correct.

Moreover if this be the true description of the whole matter it should be frankly stated, and fully established, and every one who adopts it should have the courage of his convictions and evince them by bold, clear-cut statement.

But manifestly a truth of such weighty importance should have a wider basis than one isolated passage. We should expect to see it running through the scores of passages which allude to the Pentecostal gift, and characterize most if not all. But we look in vain for this mark of genuine truth. For we have to state that, after carefully considering every allusion to this experience, and they are numbered by the hundred, we fail to find one other which will bear even a semblance of this interpretation.

For example, when the church was exhorted by the apostles to elect men to distribute their charities with even handed justice, they were directed to select men *full* of the Holy Ghost. The exhortation of the apostle was " Be *filled* with the Spirit." When a brother had erred, they that were *spiritual* were directed to restore him, not the *more* or *most* spiritual amongst the brethren —and in all the argument of the seventh and eighth chapters of Romans the contrast is between the *spiritual* man and the carnal; the man led of the Spirit being presented as a distinct, positive quantity, without variation of degree or measurement.

Now, when all other passages speak another language different from the interpretation put upon this one passage, it is in order to suspect that the interpretation is untrue to facts, and should give place to something more in harmony with the general teaching of scripture concerning this thing.

And even if the interpretation which would make it harmonize with the multitude of other scriptures should seem to be somewhat forced, it ought not to be rejected on that account, seeing the whole passage might, in the multiplicity of others, be put to one side, as obscure, without to any appreciable extent lessening the brightness of the whole Pentecostal revelation.

But again, if it be borne in mind that to be filled with the Holy Ghost, that is to give evidence of obtaining and retaining this distinct gift of God, was considered, in the early days of Christianity, as the all important matter, the fact of all facts, then the passage harmonizes with the prevailing thought, and it either is intended to draw attention to the patent fact that they who, on Pentecost, had received the gift of the Holy Ghost, had retained their Divine inhabitant and guest, and gave full or even further evidence of the fact, or it might imply that, not only those who previously had received their Pentecost, but any others who were in the company, and had not been so blessed, now received like blessing, and so they formed a company who, without exception, revelled in the one great characterizing blessing of the New Covenant.

That there is nothing strained in this explanation we point to the fact that, whilst Peter evidently received the Holy Ghost on the day of Pentecost, it is mentioned twice afterwards that he was full of the Holy Ghost, and it is not a common practice to make use of this fact to prove that between times he had parted company with the Holy Spirit or had become less spiritual.

But even if this interpretation should not receive the unqualified approval of the reader, still, we maintain, that the bare fact that there is a trace of plausibility about it, or if it suggests the possibility of any other satisfactory interpretation, taken together with the universal testimony of all other scriptures to the fact of the Pentecostal blessing being an indivisible unit, is sufficient to set aside the interpretation of the passage we are criticizing, and leave Bible utterance unmistakably clear and in perfect agreement in its testimony that to every believer this gift of the Holy Ghost is a distinct entity, is the reception of a person, in all His offices, and that there is no possibility of dividing Him up into more or less of the fulness of the Spirit. We either receive the Holy Ghost in the Pentecostal sense, or we do not, and we either walk in the Spirit or we do not, and there is no middle course indicated in God's word.

But to return to our thought that the gift of the Holy Ghost was to be the permanent characteristic of this last dispensation, we draw attention to Paul's manner of dealing with the twelve disciples whom he found at Ephesus.—Acts, ch. xix. Paul, at first thinking them to be disciples of Christ, puts to them the all-important question, evidently his standard inquiry: "Did ye receive the Holy Ghost when ye believed?"

From this question the inference is absolute, that, in Paul's estimation, they might be disciples of Christ, or believers and not have received the characteristic blessing of the New Dispensation, viz., the gift of the Holy Ghost, and, secondly, we may safely infer that two classes of believers were then recognized, viz., those who believed in Christ and had not accepted their Pentecost, and those who had.

The fact that they had not even heard of the Holy Ghost does in no sense modify these inferences. And, moreover, Paul's subsequent conduct is in perfect harmony with these deductions; for he first taught them of Christ, had them baptized in His name, and then, after they had become real disciples of Christ by all the methods provided for such change, he laid his hands on them and they received the Holy Ghost; not a part or a measure, but that distinct gift which at once linked them, in experience, with the six score disciples of Pentecost.

And this same history in these its distinguishing features may be traced in the conversion of Saul himself, on his way to Damascus, and his subsequently receiving the Holy Ghost through the ministry of Ananias, in the history of Cornelius and his friends, and the Samaritan converts.

If it be necessary to have a second marked spiritual crisis in the Christian's history then this is manifestly that experience, according to the plain, unmistakable teaching of a large number of passages in the Bible, including those above considered.

But, from our close study of the whole question, we

do not see very powerful reasons for emphasizing the fact of such necessity. For manifestly on the day of Pentecost, when thousands were added to the number of those who were rejoicing in the possession of this gift, the time between conversion and receiving the Holy Ghost was of so short duration as to be lost sight of altogether, as also in the case of the twelve Ephesian Christians. And hence we are led to the conclusion that the order of blessings was not a matter of definition, nor was a distinct period of time insisted on as necessary to intervene between the reception of the two. The all-important question, in those early times, was the fact of receiving and retaining the Heavenly guest, and methods or times were of small moment.

And fain would we see this common-sensed, apostolic state of things restored. Besides the all-important fact of possessing the gift Divine, the when or how thereof are insignificant quantities, and should by no means divide professed Christians into rival teachers or schools.

He who has marked two distinct stages in His Christian career, in securing the Pentecostal gift, and who continues to walk in Him in all the brightness of His personal presence and reign, should not narrowly criticize his brethren, to whom the passage from one stage to the other has been so rapid as to blend both pardon and the fulness of the Spirit into one bright effulgence of light, a light which in its exceeding brightness has obliterated every line of demarcation, and so *vice versa* of the other.

Wherever serious criticism, the one of the other, exists concerning this thing, the absence of the Comforter from the heart and life of the one criticizing may well be suspected.

But in vain do we look in the New Testament writings for any other well-defined epoch or crisis as generally characterizing the Christian's career. In the effort to find some other is witnessed this confusing fact, that so soon as any Scriptural term is taken hold of as distinguishing some such crisis, further reading invariably finds that term used interchangeably with conversion. This is true of sanctification, love and purity alike, and a candid reader must admit that they all, in their most pronounced forms of language, are used freely to signify the initial stage of the Christian's life.

But this vagueness of expression does not exist in connection with the gift of the Holy Ghost, for the line of demarcation between it and all other spiritual gifts is pronounced, and this clear, unmistakable isolation is carried out through a multitude of passages. Granted that there is no dogmatic creed concerning a necessary interval of time between the witness of the Spirit to sins forgiven and the Pentecostal fulness, nevertheless the distinctive characteristics of walking in the Spirit are so pronounced and so distinctly portrayed, that there is, there can be, no confusion in the mind of the sincere seeker of truth concerning the terms employed and their meaning.

CHAPTER XIV.

THE GIFT OF THE SPIRIT NECESSARILY IMPLIES COMPLETE GUIDANCE.

EVERY description of Jesus concerning the Promise of the Father, and every historical account of the Comforter received implies a *person*, who, in His spiritual presence, comes to dwell with the believer, whilst that personage, in His coming and continued abiding, is recognized in the consciousness of the one so honored.

Now when this consciousness is a practical reality, and not a mere creed or aspiration, the believer must of necessity do all things in the vivid sense of the supervision of the Spirit. Hence to walk in perfect agreement, all that is done must be agreed to or sanctioned by the guest Divine, else there is, perforce, immediate estrangement. For it is well asked in Scripture language, " How can two walk together except they be agreed ?" Walking in the Spirit must mean conscious agreement with Him in thought, word and deed.

This truth we hesitate not to assume as axiomatic—as needing no proof. Hence appears how nearly the doctrine of Divine guidance into all truth is synonymous with walking in the Spirit. And further, from this is seen how the rejection of the doctrine of guidance into all truth, or covering it up with loose generalities, accounts for the wide-spread failure, on the part of Christians, to measure up, in their lives, to apostolic experience. And also, from this aspect of the subject, a clear view of the faith which is necessary to secure and retain the Divine Comforter may be had.

Faith has been largely lost in its definitions, or overwhelmed in the multitude of its surroundings. But stripped of all these things, it stands out the simple quantity which our Lord taught men it was, so simple that he declined to define it, appealing to the consciousness of men as sufficient to testify in their hearts to what it really is.

The faith that accepts the promise of the Father, and retains the Heavenly gift, acts itself out in life, after the ordinary pattern of every day living.

The man, with money to his credit in the bank, acts out his faith in that institution by paying out his checks on the bank for what he needs, with the simple, childlike faith that his checks will be honored, and evinces no surprise if his creditor happens to notify him that his check had been cashed when presented for payment.

The person with a ten dollar bill in his pocket book, when he has faith in its genuineness, shows it by paying it across the counter for needed supplies, and is in no wise startled or surprised when it is accepted, and the overplus, if any, returned in silver or gold.

He who has perfect faith in his couch commits himself to its embrace with absolute self-abandonment, and is not surprised when it returns his confidence by sustaining his weight with ease and in security.

So also with reckless self-abandonment he flings himself upon his chair for rest, into his buggy for journeying, or into his vessel for voyaging, if he has perfect faith in their staunchness. That is, he acts as if he believed in them. But if his faith is not perfect his acts correspond, reckless self-abandonment is no longer seen, but nervous anxiety takes its place, or absolute refusal to trust his person to them.

And so, through all life's history, faith, or partial or perfect unbelief necessarily paints itself on every act.

What man in his senses would accept the faith of another as perfect in the goodness of a bank when he would hesitate to offer one of its notes in payment for goods? Who would not question the sanity of the man who pleaded poverty, and at the same time claimed to have millions in cash or real estate?

So in the kingdom of Christ, he who proclaims his poverty concerning the concomitants of the Pentecostal gift admits their necessary absence, and awakens doubt in the mind of the bearer as to the genuineness of any claim made either previously or subsequently to their possession. Indeed when any believer claims the Pentecostal gift and along with this possession uses the language of petition or aspiration which implies its lack, we are forced to believe that he is either acting a false part designedly, or else has unthinkingly drifted into habits of meaningless formality.

But he whose faith is simple and complete, that is, similar to the faith which sways him in the ordinary affairs of life, when he accepts the gift of the Holy Ghost, immediately acts out his faith in life. At once he recognizes himself as indwelt by the Holy Ghost, accepting without reserve the fact in its full significance. And moreover he at once begins to live and move in Him as a conscious presence.

Hence whatever he does he does heartily as to the Lord. When he speaks he speaks as the oracle of God. Even his thoughts are brought into captivity to the obedience of Christ.

For him to sigh for Pentecostal power in his life work, is to pour contempt on his ever present, indwelling guest and friend. To sigh for more love, or for more of the Spirit's influence is to treat the Holy Ghost with disrespect, and forfeit the confidential relations established between them.

And finally, to walk the path of life in any of its stages in doubtfulness is to let unbelief usurp the place of faith, with spiritual disaster in its train.

From all of which it follows, that to the honest disciple of Christ who has not obtained or retained the Pentecostal gift, nothing but unbelief interposes as an obstruction to the perfect realization of the crowning blessing of the New Covenant.

And further, it is evident that unbelief may give place, at any instant, to the simple faith of glad acceptance. And as that faith proves itself perfect by works, *i. e.*, by acting as if the promises of Christ were true, so the Holy Ghost in the Pentecostal sense is retained, and he walks in the Spirit, is filled with the Spirit, is led of the Spirit, in short, is no longer carnal but is a spiritual man in Christ Jesus, his body being the temple of the Holy Ghost continually.

Simple faith, in this connection, has been termed by

some recognizing the fact that the Holy Spirit is given to the believer, and his simple duty is to accept this as one of the glad facts of the gospel, and go on living and acting as if it were true, and this definition whilst not meeting the requirements of all has proved itself helpful to some.

But it will be at once seen that this faith is impossible unless there is a complete acceptance of the promises of Christ concerning the Comforter in all their fulness. It is absolutely necessary that any lingering doubt concerning one or all of them must be chased out of the soul by thorough examination of the whole subject, until the gift and work of the Holy Spirit stands or falls with the resurrection of Christ, and with nothing else.

When the mind of the believer is possessed with the truth that Christ distinctly taught that in this dispensation every believer might, at any moment, accept or recognize the Comforter as his indwelling guest, and that from that moment He would clothe him with all possible Holy Ghost power for life's work; that from that moment on He would be to him the joy and peace of Christ; that from that moment He would be to him the one and only law of life, causing him, at all times, to know and do the perfect will of God on earth, even as it is done in heaven, that is, be his constant, ever present teacher, and guide into all truth; when, we say the mind of the believer is absolutely assured of these things as most certainly promised by Christ to him as one of His sincere, honest followers in desire if not fully so in reality, then, we repeat, the truth of these things stands or falls absolutely with the resurrection of the man Christ Jesus.

For all that remains to secure perfect confidence is the assurance that He, who promised them, is able to perform. But if the resurrection of Christ Jesus is established, then His claim as to ability to make good all these things is proved beyond the shadow of a doubt, and naught remains for the honest seeker but glad acceptance, and revelling in all the possibilities and blessings comprised in this covenant of grace.

But no one will recklessly commit himself, in absolute faith, to the acceptance of all that is implied in Pentecost, whose faith is not built on the divinity of Christ, as absolutely established by His resurrection from the dead.

A creed life will accept the dicta of a church, or the traditions of a family as sufficient basis for its life. And any form of Christianity that leaves out full-orbed Pentecostal experience may rest comfortably on something short of that stupendous miracle. But he whose faith has not dug down through all creeds and traditions to the bed-rock of apostolic confidence will not walk, cannot walk in the Spirit, and prove in life what is that good and acceptable and perfect will of God.

This searching candid way of regarding the whole subject brings us at once back to the methods employed by Christ Himself; for He appealed, not to the emotions, creeds or prejudices of His hearers, but ever directed all His utterances to that inner, independent consciousness of man, which is so constituted by God Himself that by it man, if he be a lover of the truth and wills to do the will of God, may always judge righteous judgment concerning the things that pertain to his eternal welfare.

Hence He favored not snap-judgments, the outcome of emotion, or the result of popularity; but ever recommended thoughtful deliberation as that which should characterize him who would elect to be His true follower. He even seemed at times desirous of checking enthusiastic zeal, as if it gave not sufficient promise of permanency.

The impulsive, would-be follower, He pointed deliberately to the privations of His life, to be duly considered before making a decision, saying to him, "The foxes have holes, the birds of the air have nests, but the Son of Man hath not where to lay His head."

And yet He sternly denied to any a privilege which looked in the least in the direction of vacillation: "Follow me and let the dead bury their dead," was His uncompromising law to him who craved the apparently reasonable privilege of returning home to bury his father before giving himself up fully to His following.

Even the wish to return home to say farewell, in its compromising character, was pronounced a disqualifying thought in one of His disciples.

Now this cool deliberation and determined effort to examine thoroughly every step of the way of faith is to be commended, not only because of the example of Christ, but because of its reasonableness, and the vast personal interests involved, yes, and the interests of mankind ever appeal to us as largely involved in our individual action concerning this thing.

And therefore every motive and every sacred interest that can centre in man makes its separate claim to be heard, and all combined demand, with a dignity that a background of eternal consequences heightens, that each and every one should sit down and examine this subject to its foundation, with a carefulness and sincere love of the truth that will stand the searching investigations of the judgment day.

For, we maintain, that the benefits of Pentecost are not *now* so much the outcome of faith as of knowledge, connected with love of the truth; for where these exist, faith will follow as a natural, if not a necessary consequence. Therefore the whole subject appeals most forcibly to all to search into it, as for hidden treasure, and applies its whip and spur to urge on the seeking one till certain knowledge is obtained, a knowledge that will formulate itself in clear-cut statement, whether it be favorable or adverse to the full claims of the passage, "He will guide you into all truth," and with the understanding that to rest in the half truths which hide behind generalized statement is the perdition of ungodly men, who are not willing to receive the truth in the love of it, and so court the delusion that believes a lie, to their condemnation. (See 2 Thess. ii. 12.)

CHAPTER XV.

SIMPLICITY RESTORED.

IT is marvellous what simplicity is brought into doctrinal teaching when Pentecost is seen to take this practical, workable form. The mysticism which is the true child of uncertainty is banished forever.

For a close analyst of the writings of the mystics will ever discover that in their minds there was a fugitive something, which, like the philosopher's stone, was considered of supreme excellence, and to obtain which all their rules and ascetic practices had their birth and being. But unlike the philosopher's stone or the fancied elixir of life, glimpses of it were now and then obtained, and occasionally lengthened possession. But generally the experience of it was according to the following extract from Bernard, which is quoted approvingly by Flavel:

"It is a sweet hour, and it is but an hour—a thing of short continuance—the relish of it is exceeding sweet, but it is not often that Christians taste it."

Now we maintain that this air of uncertainty runs through all their writings, and gives them a sombre, weird character, which both attracts and repels. Backed by the saintly character of the writers, and showing traces of Pentecostal fulness of blessing, they command our respect, and at times feed our innate longings after perfection of character and life.

But their unnaturalness and indefiniteness affect us like a narrative charged with the supernatural, and we seem to breathe more freely, and to secure a kind of regained freedom, when we come from under their spell into the garish light of ordinary every day life.

We maintain that the major part of these writings would shrivel up into a pious ejaculation of holy horror at the bare mention of the thought that every Christian, at any stage of his experience, might accept the Holy Ghost in Pentecostal fulness, and, from that point of time, live on in the constant possession of the peace of God which passeth all understanding, the fulness of joy in the Holy Ghost, and have the abiding witness of the Spirit that every moment of every year thereafter he walked worthy of God unto all pleasing. Or in other words, that he might ever after live before God and man the best possible life for him to live.

For before this vigorous, practical statement, their whole ponderous superstructure of recommendations concerning mortifying the flesh, concerning crucifying the affections and inclinations, concerning absence from society for prayer, silence or recollection, are dissipated into mists, the home of phantoms, mists that so soon as this statement is received as the teaching of Christ and his apostles, disappear completely, even as the exhalations of earth flee away before the rising sun.

For if it is true that when the Holy Ghost is received in the full-orbed, Pentecostal sense, that is, to walk in Him as the one and only law of life, and when as a necessary consequence it is seen that righteousness, peace and joy in Him is the constant experience of such an one, it follows that there is absolutely no place for any of all the mystic practices for growth in grace, which imply, in their use, the slightest lack in any direction.

That growth in grace which is the outcome of human effort, even if that effort manifests itself in such simple acts as enforced silence, is in its essence opposed to the very genius of Christianity.

For the idea of growth, in the scriptural sense, is ever associated with perfection, in the *moment* of growth. Therefore the growth which connects itself with present imperfection is conceived in human thought, and must, in the nature of the case, give rise to unhealthy monstrous *growths*, which, in their peculiarities, contrast with the perfect symmetrical growth of Christian perfection.

For if one possesses the peace of God which passes all understanding the growth of that peace, if possible, must be according to the laws of God's peace. And the same must be said with respect to joy in the Holy Ghost, whilst that righteousness which is in the Spirit, and walks *worthy* of God, cannot be enhanced by any tricks of voluntary humility.

That there is growth, in the *kingdom of God* within such a believer, does not follow from any reasonings concerning its nature or necessities, but is a positive revelation of God, and therefore must, in the nature of the case, be realized by every one who by faith accepts this Christian perfection of character and life.

Hence it follows that the first requisite for growth in grace is momentary perfection in Christian life, when growth follows as a Divine necessity, and after the Divine pattern.

Whence it also follows that the faith which accepts the Holy Ghost in the Pentecostal sense, and which momentarily walks in the Spirit, is the Alpha and Omega of all efforts to grow in grace. We repeat the thought, that this practical business-like statement of Pentecostal truth drives away the last vestige of mysticism from the gospel, and allays all fear of its reappearing, excepting to those who turn away from the simplicity of the gospel because of their want of love for the truth.

So, too, before this Pentecostal truth the spirit of Antinomianism must quail, and, however bold in its onset, must eventually fly before it. For the lurking desire of Antinomianism is to condone sin. Conscious of inability to keep the whole law of God in thought, word and deed, it labors to establish a righteousness which will be acceptable to God, and satisfactory to men, without enduring the rigid test of holy living.

Hence the semi-mystical doctrines concerning imputed righteousness, standing in Christ, two records, one on earth and one in heaven, and the far-reaching result of intellectual faith; the teaching of all which is that a man may from time to time be the prey of evil thoughts, the mouthpiece of improper words, and the author of lustful acts, and yet be pure and holy in the sight of God.

But as contrasted to all this, Pentecostal truth demands that the righteousness of the law be *fulfilled* in us, who walk not after the flesh but after the Spirit. That is, that not only the letter but also the intention of all law should be fulfilled in the life of the believer who walks in the Spirit.

Moreover it points to Christ and the apostles as illustrations of this kind of righteous living. Now Christ appealed to the multitude to test His life by the written laws of the Bible, and the law of God written in their consciousness: "Which of you convinceth me of sin?" implied this challenge to all men. Even to the man who, at His trial, struck Him with his hand Jesus said, "If I have spoken evil bear witness of the evil," plainly implying that He refused not to be arraigned before the tribunal of the world's conscience.

Moreover He declared that the intention of His gospel was to enable man to fulfil the whole law, " Verily I say unto you one jot or tittle shall in no wise pass from the law till all be fulfilled," evidently teaches this stringent requirement, for it is immediately added, as a commentary thereto, that whosoever should break one of the least of the commandments should be adjudged guilty.

And Paul, in the spirit of this teaching, challenged whole churches to judge of his life as lived in conformity to the laws of God.

James, in his epistle, labors to make it evident that the outcome of the gospel must be that the real, spiritual Christian, who walks in the Spirit, might safely challenge the justice of God concerning the outward expression of that life. "Ye see then how that by works a man is *justified* and not by faith only."—James ii. 24.

John is equally emphatic in pronouncing on all outward forms of sin as having their origin from the devil, and as such rendering the one practising them a partaker of his evil nature. "He that doeth righteousness is righteous, even as He (Christ) is righteous; He that committeth sin is of the devil," is an unmistakably plain deliverance concerning this thing.

And here we remark that had the simplicity of Pentecostal truth been preserved, there would have been no temptation to dress up this Antinomian monster in Christian garments. For the righteousness of the law being practically fulfilled in the life, there would have been no felt need anywhere to harmonize Bible teaching with an imperfect life.

Walking in the Spirit, in the Pentecostal sense, secures such a common-sensed, practical obedience to all the commands of God, that it invites the examination of man and angel to judge of its excellence, not by occult, mystical rules concerning imputed righteousness, and one's standing in Christ, but by all laws of God, whether written on the heart, or in the sacred canon of Truth. Therefore in the presence of this life, which is the outcome of walking in the Spirit, God is honored and Antinomianism slinks away into its loved darkness.

But not only are the more pronounced forms of this error rebuked, but also the milder or more subtle ramifications of the evil are exposed, for, wherever an imperfect life exists, however strong the Christian testimony, and however clear and scriptural the creed, there is ever a leaning to some form of Antinomian teaching.

It matters not if this conscious defect in the life is considered absolutely unavoidable, still the patent fact that there is a discrepancy between the life and the standard of holy living which Christ has set up, unconsciously calls for some form of doctrine which will bridge over the chasm.

Now the teachings of Christ call for a life which will be a complete pattern of His own, in all its manward aspects, or else His words cannot be made to appeal to the ordinary, common-sensed judgment of mankind— "Be ye therefore perfect as your Father which is in heaven is perfect;" "Thy will be done on earth as it is done in heaven;" "Thou shalt love the Lord thy God with all thy heart,—and—thy neighbor as thyself," are specimens of this thought, and specimens of the whole trend of His teaching.

And apostolic utterance is but an emphatic endorsation of this thought, as the beginning, middle and end of His gospel.

Now, however high the claims of the saint in holy living, if they fall short of this exalted standard, there is a feeling of uneasiness which instinctively seizes upon any form of teaching which makes a plausible claim to meet this difficulty. And hence we account for the tendency of the majority of all formulated creeds concerning holy living to be more or less permeated with this Antinomian spirit.

In this connection we are forced to indict much of what is taught and written on such subjects as carnality, inbred sin, sin in believers, theories concerning temptations, different degrees of love, purity and power, and similar subjects in endless variety of detail. And as these are burning questions of the present day, we feel that no apology is due the reader in undertaking to examine into them carefully and minutely.

CHAPTER XVI.

CARNALITY.

WHEN a sinner comes to Christ in confession and faith he is accepted, pardoned and adopted into the kingdom of God's Son. This is an accepted truth, not only by Methodists, but also by all evangelical churches, accepted because it is believed to be in thorough harmony with Bible teaching.

But this adopted child of God is now an heir of heaven, and prepared for all the felicities thereof should he at once be overtaken by death.

This fact of the pardoned and adopted sinner gaining heaven should he die in this gracious state is accepted by all modern theologians, including the Wesleys and their adherents; yes, and without his having consciously experienced a second blessing whereby carnality, or inbred sin, has been destroyed.

It is true that some writers, including Wesley, seem to teach the contrary, for instance, when they comment on the verse, "Without holiness no man shall see the Lord." But when brought to face the question squarely, they all admit, without one dissenting voice, that when a sinner is pardoned and regenerated, if he should die the next moment he is certain to gain heaven.

Now it is plain, when this is a universally accepted fact, that all theories or teachings concerning carnality and inbred sin must be made to harmonize with this fact. John Wesley saw this, and met it, as we might expect, without any attempt to go around the difficulty, and fitted his theory to this admitted fact, in this way. He maintained that if a Christian was clearly regenerated when dying, but was not entirely sanctified, that is, had not experienced the second change whereby inbred sin was destroyed, that in this case God cut the work short in righteousness, and made an end of sin in him at the last moment or moments of his life, and so he entered heaven both as regenerated and entirely sanctified. And this reasoning is adopted by most holiness writers on this subject.

If any one is asked to produce Scripture for this teaching, it has to be confessed that there is none, but that it is purely an inference, the result of a reasoning process.

Some impatient one, perhaps, here asks, Do you accept this solution of the difficulty as absolutely correct? We reply that, as to all the facts, we are in harmony with Wesley's teaching, for those facts are in harmony with the Bible; that is to say, with him we believe that the depravity of the human heart is a positive fact; that confession of sin and faith in Christ secure pardon and regeneration; moreover, with Wesley we believe that it is possible for a man to receive all that is implied in conversion and sanctification at first, and thereafter live the life of Christian perfection.

But, with him, we have failed to find one instance of this in actual life. As a general fact, men after conversion live in a state where alternate sinning and repenting chase each other like clouds in the sky. And with him we believe that this state, which he sometimes denominated the wilderness state, may give place to one where the believer walks constantly worthy of God unto all pleasing. These are the facts of the case which Wesley received, because found in the Bible, and observed in life.

Now it was and is to these facts of Bible truth which are brought out in Wesley's teaching that we, as a Methodist minister, subscribed and still loyally defend as the very foundation of Scriptural holiness. But as to methods of stating these truths, and arguments and inferences used by him in their elucidation, no sane person could feel it obligatory on him to accept all as ultimate truth, or that it would be wrong to let one's thoughts concerning these facts take any other course than the methods and reasonings Wesley used.

We, therefore, simply give Wesley's method of making the doctrine of carnality in believers harmonize with the facts of the case as a matter of theological history. We certainly think it improvable, or we would not write on the subject.

Now, we ask, is it not in order to seek for some method whereby all Scripture statement concerning carnality can be harmonized with facts, without getting into difficulty over a regenerate person dying without having experienced the further work of grace known as full salvation?

For many years we fully appreciated this weakness in the modern theory concerning inbred sin, and as we could find no satisfactory solution for the difficulty, we simply laid the whole matter aside, and took a short cut to the experience of holiness itself, and left this and kindred theories growing out of it to be considered in after years, if at all.

But now that we have met a solution of the whole matter, in the Bible, which satisfies us, as not only in harmony with Scripture, but also with the facts of experience, yes, and with Wesley's teaching, we hesitate no longer to discourse about it.

This is what we now think to be the simple teaching of the Scriptures concerning this thing. When the sinner comes to Christ with confession, and accepts Him by faith as his Saviour, he is at once pardoned and accepted as His follower, the Holy Spirit witnesses to the fact of his pardon and acceptance, and thus He knows, with infallible certainty, that he is an adopted child of God, an heir of heaven.

Now, his first impulse is to love and serve God with all his ransomed powers. At this point the Holy Spirit undertakes to lead him into all truth, and be to him all that Christ promised him to be. And it is possible for this believer to accept the rich provision made for all his spiritual needs, and go on his way rejoicing, without one moment's break in his experience of freedom from condemnation for sin.

But, as a matter of history, all, sooner or later, undertake to live the Christian life without walking in the Spirit—that is, without distinctly accepting Him as the sole law of life in all things great and small, and, of necessity, live a sinning and repenting life, that is, if they do not speedily turn away altogether from the effort to live godly.

Now, this attempt to walk in the commandments and ordinances of the Bible, without making the Spirit the one law of life, is what the Apostle denominates carnality, the flesh, or the old man, and it is in essence, the same as those efforts put forth before conversion to avoid sin and lead a righteous life.

But when the believer accepts the Holy Spirit in the Pentecostal sense, that is, to obey Him as the sole rule of life, then in this, his walk in the Spirit, he illustrates the scriptural idea of a blameless, holy life, where carnality is destroyed, the old man crucified, or, which is the same thing, John Wesley's idea of Christian perfection.

The objection may be made that this effort to do what is right seems worthy of commendation, whilst carnality is pictured as all bad, the very essence of evil. How then, it may be asked, can these apparent contrasts be similar?

But it will be noticed that Paul maintains that all efforts put forth to keep the law, when the person is not led of the Spirit, end in failure. Hence, all allusions to such efforts necessarily imply sin as the inevitable result. So that when he speaks of one he includes the other.

As a matter of fact, all men without exception strive to keep the law of God. No man out of perdition is absolutely bad. Who ever met a drunken sot, for example, so far gone in sin that he did not now and then put forth some feeble efforts to stem the torrent of sin in him? Even the most profligate and unholy are restrained somewhat by conscience against the bent of natural desire. So we contend that sin, whether committed by professed saint or open sinner, is aptly described, or at all events is included, in an allusion to the efforts of men to keep the law of God without obeying the law of the Spirit.

How all disputes concerning the application of Paul's

reasonings in the seventh and eighth chapters of Romans are ended when this key is used to unlock their mysteries!

St. Paul is describing all efforts to keep the law of God without adopting Heaven's provision for keeping it in its entirety. In so doing it is not necessary for him to make nice points concerning inbred sin and open transgressions; concerning infirmities and mistakes, whether regrettable or otherwise; concerning sins of omission or commission, as to whether they are voluntary or involuntary, as is necessary with modern writers in upholding their theories.

No, nor yet was it necessary for Paul to mention the fact as to whether he was describing his own experience before or after conversion. If we regard him as simply describing all efforts to keep the law of God when not *walking after the Spirit,* that is, when not obeying the law of the Spirit as the only law of life, then we can understand why it was unnecessary for him to guard against the theological discussions which have so thickened about these chapters. He was simply giving a vivid description of every son and daughter of Adam when not walking in the Spirit, or when not living the life portrayed in the eighth chapter.

In the seventh chapter you have man at his very best, when not led of the Spirit. You see a man putting forth all possible effort to keep the laws of God, and finally giving up in absolute despair of ever succeeding.

Now, it is of importance that we should know what it was that this representative man despaired of. We maintain that his despair was not concerning his inability to secure forgiveness so much as his inability to keep the law of God. This the whole trend of the argument shows, and is brought out with clearness in individual passages. "There is, therefore, now no condemnation to them that are in Christ Jesus, who walk not after the flesh but after the Spirit," speaks of freedom from condemnation, not because of forgiveness and cleansing, but because sin is not committed, which fact is more fully asserted further on, " the righteousness of the law is fulfilled in us who walk after the Spirit."

These, we repeat, are the facts brought out in the apostle's grand description or argument concerning the two states, viz., that all efforts to fulfil the righteousness of the law without following the law, or guidance of the Spirit, as the one and only law of life, end in failure, and man in so acting is *carnal*, the *old man* not being dead or crucified. But so soon as he begins to walk in the Spirit, then sin ceases in him, and so long as he so walks, even as Christ walked, he has no condemnation for sin, seeing he does not commit sin.

CHAPTER XVII.
CARNALITY CONTINUED.

CLEANSING, OR HEART PURITY.—In connection with the discussion of carnality, it is in order to investigate thoroughly this subject. But it will be found, on close inspection, that it can be quickly and easily disposed of, for the state of being cleansed, or of having a pure heart, is simply another name or names for a righteous life. A man of clean hands, and of a pure heart, is simply a man whose hands are not used in wrong-doing, and whose life in thought, word and deed harmonizes with the commands of God; in other words, is one in whose conduct the righteousness of the law is continually fulfilled.

These hands are clean, cries the politician, when he would have his audience believe that he neither gave nor accepted a bribe. There is no mysticism connected with the word clean and its synonyms outside of *theology*. But the moment we enter the realms of dogmatic theology we seem to be on enchanted ground, especially when the cleansing department is reached. For it will be found that walking in the commandments of God blameless can scarcely be considered as synonymous with the idea of being cleansed from inborn or inbred sin, as taught by many theological writers, when discoursing concerning holiness.

Take an object lesson to illustrate this. Here is a man converted to God. About his conversion there is no doubt. He has sincerely repented of his sins, has come to God in penitence and faith, and has accepted Jesus as the Captain of his salvation. There is no reserve in his complete surrender to Him as the one whom he promises to love and obey now and forever. As a consequence his load of guilt is lifted, he has now light and joy in his soul, and the clear, unmistakable witness of the Holy Spirit that he is an accepted child of God, an heir of Heaven. In short, that he is born again of the Spirit, and so sees the kingdom of Heaven—that is, belongs to it.

He is now, at the close of his first day in this spiritual kingdom, about to retire for needed sleep. With his heart overflowing with thanksgiving because of the conscious forgiveness of all his past sins, and with such a sense of present satisfaction in Christ that precludes even the suspicion of having been disloyal to the Saviour, by the commission of one sin since his conversion a few hours ago, which needed confession and forgiveness, happy in God he drops into slumber, and, ere the morrow dawns, drops into eternity.

Now the question is, Was this man cleansed from all sin before he went to sleep? Did he live a pure and holy life between his conversion and his first sleep, which proved to be the sleep of death?

To us it is clear that if cleansing means right doing, that is, walking in the commandments blameless, then he lived during those few hours a pure, holy life. But if it means something over and above holy living, then it is in order to show clearly and unmistakably what that overplus something is.

Let us look at some of the confused efforts to show what that assumed something is. It is asserted that if this individual had lived long enough, the inborn or inbred sin which was still in him would soon have begun to show itself in various forms, as, for instance, risings of temper, evil thoughts, infirmities of will; in short, after a time he would discover in his life sins of omission, if not of commission, needing, ever and anon, confession and forgiveness, till he obtained the blessing of heart purity, when inbred sin being taken out, nothing but pure love to God would remain. Hence it is argued that the seed of sin, that is, original depravity, was not taken out of him at conversion, it was only kept down out of sight.

Now we admit the facts of the case as here brought out. It is all but certain that had this individual lived and striven, after the ordinary way, to live a holy life, he would have met with many a failure, no matter how intense his efforts in that direction. But not, we maintain, because of some defective work done in his being by the great Author of his salvation, but because the probabilities are that he would fail to accept the Holy Ghost in a Pentecostal sense, and so, not adopting the divine provision fully for fulfilling the righteousness of the law, he would necessarily fail, and so live a sinning and repenting life if he continued his efforts after holy living.

The apostles did not raise subtle questions about inbred or inborn sin in dealing with their converts, but confined themselves to seeing that they accepted the Holy Ghost in the Pentecostal sense, and then walked in

Him, that is, obeyed Him as the one and only law of life, well knowing that thus the righteousness of the law would be fulfilled in them perfectly.

We challenge any modern teacher to improve on the apostolic method as exemplified in the history of the twelve Ephesian disciples. And, moreover, we challenge any and all dogmatic teachers concerning the blessing of purity to take the position that these twelve needed to to be cleansed from inborn or inbred sin after they had received the Holy Ghost.

When the plain, legitimate meaning of the terms, cleansing and heart purity, is retained, viz., keeping the commandments of God in their entirety, then, not only no damage comes from the use of them, but they increase the pleasing variety of expressions which indicate holy living.

But when, as is too often the case, they are used to condone sin, and bolster up a form of teaching that is semi-Antinomian in its make, then it is in order to ask if it is not better to discard their use, or make them less prominent for a time, till the evil effects of the abuse of the terms cease.

Need we add that this abuse is witnessed when they are made to imply that some mysterious change is continually passing over the soul of him who believes that the blood cleanseth, whereby he is reckoned holy and pure in the sight of God, even although he does not do the will of God on earth as it is done in Heaven?

SANCTIFICATION AND ENTIRE SANCTIFICATION.— In connection with the subject of carnality, it will also be well to comment on the above expressions.

Now, in using the same methods as in previous writings, if we connect these terms with the real facts in Christian experience, the sense of confused thought, engendered by the use of them, is somewhat lessened.

Certainly, at the outset, we must admit that there is a confusion of ideas suggested by this nomenclature. For it implies the possibility of comparing absolute terms, and so brings up the old dispute as to whether perfect and kindred words admit of comparison as, *perfect, more perfect, most perfect*. Accurate scholarship demands that Christ's comments on the words *yea* and *nay* be applied to all words implying completeness or perfection, teaching, as they do, that whatsoever is more than the positive degree cometh of evil.

With a good-natured smile even grammarians will let pass the rivalries of charlatans in the business world who, to catch the eye of the purchaser, tack on their limitless superlatives, as, "very best," "better than the best," "still better than the very best," and so on *ad nauseam*. And so it comes to pass that the scholarly infidel, with some apparent ground for his act, classes the nomenclature concerning sanctification not with accurate speech, but with charlatanism.

We are fully aware that some good people will be conscious of a species of holy horror taking possession of them at seeing these terms handled after this commonsense, business way. For when any terms of speech are associated for a long time with a sacred subject, the very words gather around them a kind of sacredness, and he is rightly termed an iconoclast who dares to handle them with any other than a superstitious reverence for the very letters of which they are composed.

As for us, we frankly admit that we have no such sentiment concerning these terms. For the word sanctify, and its derivations, in the Bible is applied alike to men, animals, and inanimate objects, whilst the expression *entire sanctification* is not even a scriptural one. True, it is supposed to be perfectly synonymous with the expression, "sanctify you wholly." But it is a legitimate dispute whether this expression, addressed by St. Paul to a whole Church, was intended by him to be applicable to single individuals.

Once it was not so; for we distinctly remember with what awe we first used the expression entire sanctification when, from a sense of duty, we used it as expressing our personal experience of full salvation, and by this token we are persuaded that it bears like awe-inspiring thoughts to many minds.

But the question may be on the poise in the reader's mind, waiting a break in the argument, Do you think the expression entire sanctification, as used in modern holiness literature, objectionable? Certainly we do think it to be decidedly unfortunate, because calculated to mislead.

Let any one lay aside his acquired reverence for the expression, and then apply to it the ordinary commonsensed examination which is applied to other things to learn their true value, and see how soon the objections to its use accumulate.

Now the word sanctified means *set apart, separated to a holy use.* If then anything is thus set apart, can there be any difference between its being *simply* set apart, and *entirely* set apart? Both expressions must mean exactly the same thing, or else the first one is not truthful.

Or if the general meaning attached to the term be taken, viz., to be *cleansed or made pure or holy*, entire sanctification cannot possibly convey any additional meaning to the word sanctified.

So we maintain, that every way considered, the expression is an awkward one, and must, in the nature of things, tend to confusion of ideas.

But do you not believe in entire sanctification? one asks. Yes, surely we believe in the fact which Wesley used this redundant expression to indicate. And would that modern holiness teachers indicated as clearly as he did the scriptural idea of walking in the Spirit, and there would follow from its use less evil than is witnessed at the present time.

But to make more evident the unfitness of this expression for its intended purpose, take an object lesson. Here is a leader of a religious service who wishes to have sinners converted and believers brought into the experience indicated by this term. To be consistent, he should ask the unconverted forward to be *sanctified*, and the other classes to be *entirely sanctified*.

Imagine the perplexity of those at the altar in planning how to take *two* steps in sanctifying themselves or appropriating Christ as their santification! And what bewilderment might be in the minds of the seekers of entire sanctification, in apparently admitting that when they first came to Christ they did not separate themselves fully to Him, or did not entirely accept Christ as their sanctification. And the bewilderment is further intensified, in that their Master apparently accepted their partial consecration, and gave them the power for a time, at least, to become real sons of God, without rebuke.

Again, it is a suggestive thought in this connection that this expression is founded on but one scripture reference, as far as we have been able to learn; and that one, as we above remarked, by no means clearly and positively sanctioning it. We have learned to be somewhat shy of expressions with such slight scriptural basis.

LOVE AND PERFECT LOVE.—This subject of carnality would not be complete without an extended consideration of *love* in this connection.

If this word be examined in its relation to the whole subject indicated, it will be found that its meaning has been left in a very perplexing state.

For example, different states or degrees of love in the same individual are made to stand for the two blessings of justification and sanctification, but no clear definition is given of these different shades or degrees of love.

Certain Scriptures are quoted for this discrimination, and the writings of Wesley and others are made to do service here. And it is evident that these two degrees of love seem to be indicated by them. But what that difference is, is left in doubt. "He that feareth is not made *perfect* in love." 1 John iv. 18, plainly intimates that a man may love and yet not be perfect in his love; "and His love is perfected in us." 1 John iv. 12 seems to speak the same language.

These are the only passages with which we are familiar, that appear to bear out the thought that there is one degree of love present in the soul that is only justified, and another in the sanctified. Of course, when we take up the writings of modern teachers on this subject, they abound in statements of this kind.

Now, granted all that is contended for concerning this thing, see in what confusion of thought the whole matter is left. For the command to love God perfectly is as emphatic in the Old Testament as in the New. Now, one of the favorite arguments used to prove the ability on our part of loving God perfectly is that it is commanded that we should so love Him, and the command itself implies that provision has been made for our obedience. Therefore, it follows that provision was made for the Israelite of old to love God perfectly, as certainly as for the Christian of to-day. Hence, if perfect love characterizes the blessing of entire sanctification, then there can be no essential difference concerning it in the two dispensations. How, then, make good Paul's description, when he says that the one had no glory in comparison with the other.

Again, since under both dispensations we are commanded to love God perfectly, how can God be just and the justifier of any man who does not so love God perfectly? It would seem that perfect love is made a necessity on our part, even in the very first steps in a Christian life.

Again, in the same chapter from which the above quotations have been taken, John discourses as if there were not those degrees in love, for he saith that "every one that *loveth* is born of God and knoweth God. He that loveth not knoweth not God; for God is love."

But it may be said that he is discoursing here concerning perfect love. Granted, then he is made by this admission to exclude all who do not love after this sort from the kingdom of Christ. And applying that thought to the former verses quoted, it would make them say that he that was not made perfect in love was not born of God and knew not God. Manifestly, then, it would make the subject abound in difficulties to fit the two states of justification and sanctification to these utterances of the great apostle of love.

That these, and a multitude of similar difficulties abound in this subject, when considered after the modern method, any one who honestly questions himself must admit. But generally this perplexity is gotten over by a pious ejaculation as, O for more love! and the whole subject is again relegated to the *limbo* of unsettled questions.

Do we propose to settle this unsolved problem? Well, seeing it is manifestly an unsettled one, no one should find fault at an honest attempt in that direction.

We are inclined to think that the entire difficulty has originated in the effort to deal with love as an abstract, and not as a concrete, quantity. That is, love is looked at too much as an emotion, and not as an act. It will be noticed, if the mind is turned to this thought, that in the Bible the acts of life are referred to more than the emotions when this subject is mentioned. Read carefully the epistle from which the above quotations are made, and this contention will be easily established. "But whoso keepeth His Word, in him, verily, is the love of God perfected." "My little children, let us not love in word, neither in tongue; but in deed and in truth." "For this is the love of God, that we keep his commandments."

Again, Jesus Himself gave the same description of love. "He that hath My commandments, and keepeth them, he it is that loveth Me." And similar passages are scattered through every part of the Bible.

Hence, it follows that he who keeps the commands of Christ need not be troubled about the different shades of love, for his love, according to the Bible, is complete and satisfactory to his God. But any who do not keep perfectly the commandments of Christ, whilst they cannot lay claim to *perfect* love toward God and man, may well fear concerning their standing before God in any relation that can be either satisfactory to themselves or their Master.

Now, take this thought thus plainly brought out, and see how it will explain the experiences of Christians. Here is a man just converted to God from a life of sin. It is a genuine conversion; he has, without any reserve, accepted Christ as his Saviour now and forever, with the intention to follow Him loyally in all things. Now, watch him for the first few hours or days of his changed life, and see if there is any defect in his obedience to all the commandments of Christ. Usually you find none. That is, he is fully up to the mark, walking in all the commands and ordinances of God blameless. If you doubt it, just charge him with want of loyal obedience to his Saviour, and see how he will indignantly refuse to be condemned by your accusation. Again, accuse him of not loving God with all his heart, and see how, concerning this thing, he will maintain his integrity. And even if your accusation drives him to his Master for vindication, notice how he will tell of love tokens given him to confirm him in this his faith.

Reader, is not this an accurate description of the first hours or days of your Christian life? Alas, for you if it is not

Now, if all this be admitted, and we hesitate not to demand its admission, then, according to clear scriptural definition, the newly converted child of God loves Him perfectly; that is, with all his heart, mind, soul, and strength. And, if he goes on from that glad hour in continued obedience, then, notwithstanding all the reasonings of modern holiness writers to the contrary, according to Bible testimony, he lives a life of perfect love toward God and man.

But, does he thus go on in perfect obedience? Alas, no. How rare the instances! So rare, that the existence of one living example, one who for years after his conversion has such a record, is doubted by most, if not all. And why? Because the provision made for perfect, continuous obedience has been almost universally rejected.

But, when the Holy Ghost is received in the Pentecostal sense, that is, to be the one and only law of life, then this Christian, in his implicit walk in the Spirit, obeys perfectly all the commands of God, and so fulfils all the conditions of perfect, continual love toward God and man.

Now, if this state of final establishment be called the blessing of perfect love, in contrast with that intermittent state which usually precedes it, where, through ignorance of the Spirit's work, He, the Spirit, only for short periods of time after each act of forgiveness has right-of-way in the soul of the believer, then the confusion of ideas connected with the modern method of treating the subject of love in connection with the doctrine of holiness would cease.

Let us, then, gather up the results of this discussion, as follows:

Whilst the Bible proclaims as a universal fact that he that loves God keeps His commandments, it is still more pronounced in the statement that he that keeps the commandments loves God.

If there is any place in Christian experience for two distinctive degrees of love, as *love* and *perfect love*, it must be when fitful obedience is contrasted with continued, perfected obedience.

These two states can only be accounted for when, either through ignorance, lack of faith, or defective teaching, the law of the Spirit as the only law of life is not an accepted fact in one's Christian experience. That is when believers do not receive the Holy Ghost, or, having received Him, do not continue to walk in Him

And further, it is seriously hinted at, if not fully proclaimed, in the Bible, that defective obedience, at least where the conscience is affected, is a sure sign of the absence in the heart of any true love towards God.

CHAPTER XVIII.

SCRIPTURALNESS OF THIS TEACHING.

WHEN such a departure from the ordinary way of presenting these truths is witnessed, there is naturally a call to examine with renewed care their foundations, and this call is the same as asking, Is it Scriptural?

Some take their stand on one or two passages in the Bible and maintain against all comers that one isolated sentence in the Holy Scriptures is quite sufficient to establish any doctrine. Hence whole sects are founded on the interpretation of one or two passages, and entire schools of thought pivot on a single expression.

Take the verse which contains the words "Sanctify you wholly" from the New Testament, and the expression *entire sanctification* would have no *apparent* warrant in Holy Writ. Eliminate the one passage from the Epistle of James with its bearing on the Faith Cure movement, and the extreme views put forward by some of the leaders thereof would scarcely have seen the light. Let the two and only two passages which appear to give definite teaching concerning dress be lost sight of, and all the ponderous rules and regulations concerning dress, in connection with holiness, could hardly have had a birth. And so of other doctrines which might be mentioned.

Now whilst admitting that any utterance that can be fairly traced to Christ, the last ultimate teacher of truth, is sufficient to establish its correctness, we suggest that, where clashing views obtain, if numerous passages can be collected, that an important argument can be based on the number of these passages, as contrasted with the paucity of those which seem to support rival schools of thought.

Napoleon gave it as his decided opinion that victory always followed the largest battalions. Now whilst this is not always true, nevertheless it suggests a general truth. And hence it is in order to see how, in the New Testament, the passages which refer to the gift of the Holy Ghost compare with those which refer to *heart purity, entire sanctification,* holiness, or perfect love as a second blessing subsequent to or apart from forgiveness of sins.

Now if the reader should take his New Testament and go carefully over the whole, as we have done, and mark every passage which has reference to any one of these five different subjects, he would verify, we think, the following as correct, viz.:

	No. of times mentioned.
Perfect Love,	3
Cleansing,	9
Sanctification,	16
Holiness,	87
The Gift of the Holy Ghost,	156
Indirect allusions to entire Sanctification,	1
" " " Cleansing,	2
" " " the Pentecostal Gift,	76

These figures might possibly elicit a dispute concerning their accuracy, in a few instances, but as giving a bird's-eye view of the relative importance attached to the subjects mentioned, we claim them to be sufficiently accurate to found our argument upon them.

Now it will be noticed that the passages marked as alluding to holiness and sanctification apply as certainly to the Pentecostal gift, as they do to heart purity, entire sanctification, or perfect love, when they are made to have reference to a distinctive blessing, and so they do not count in this comparison. Hence the relative value in the estimation of the writers of the New Testament, of the gift of the Holy Ghost in the Pentecostal sense as compared with those other subjects is upwards of one hundred and fifty to nine, as compared with the subject of cleansing; to three as compared with perfect love; and to less than one as compared with entire sanctification.

But if the passages themselves be examined into more minutely, it will be seen that, whilst those which refer to the gift of the Holy Ghost do so in the main as to a distinctive something which can only be intelligibly interpreted by Pentecost, the other passages are not nearly so distinctive in their teaching.

The first of the nine passages referring to cleansing is in Acts xv. 8: "And made no distinction between us and them, cleansing their hearts by faith."

The usual interpretation here is that cleansing refers to the distinctive blessing received by Cornelius and his friends whilst Peter was preaching to them. Now, granted this, even then the subordinate nature of the expression is shown, for this is the third allusion to the same event, and in all three it is particularly mentioned as the giving or receiving the Holy Ghost in the Pentecostal sense, and only in this third passage is cleansing named.

But we ask, would it strain the passage to make cleansing here refer to their subsequent lives, in which they were kept pure, that is, obedient to the laws of God by faith in the presence and guidance of the Spirit? Especially when it is borne in mind that the controversy mentioned in this chapter was not about receiving a blessing of purity, but being kept pure.

There was no dispute about the reception of the blessing, whatever name might be given to it, the whole controversy was about the subsequent life. Some insisted on the necessity of these Gentile converts keeping the law in order to maintain their standing with God, whilst others opposed this as contrary to the spirit of the Gospel.

We do not contend for this meaning of the passage as if it was of vital importance; it is sufficient for our argument to show that one cannot dogmatize safely concerning the usual application of this solitary passage concerning cleansing in the Acts of the Apostles.

But in this book of the Acts, whilst they, who insist on the blessing of a clean heart being the true scriptural name for full salvation, find only this one mention of the subject, forty-nine passages will be found, all pointing with distinctiveness to the gift of the Holy Ghost as the true name for the full salvation of the New Dispensation.

In Romans we find no verse which by ordinary ingenuity can be made to express the doctrine of heart purity as the second blessing. But twenty-six tell of the gift of the Holy Ghost as indicating it.

In 1 Cor. vi. 11, the next passage occurs, which reads: "But ye were washed, but ye were sanctified, but ye were justified in the name of the Lord Jesus Christ, and in the Spirit of our God." But a glance at the verse will suggest innumerable difficulties in using this passage in the interests of cleansing as the second blessing, for it is either put on a par with justification or made inferior to it by being made to come before it.

But when the evident meaning of the verse has right of way in the mind there is no confusion in it, for it points to the forgiveness or washing away of past sins, the sanctification or setting apart to the service of God, and living a just or holy life as all coming to them through Christ in the gift of the Holy Ghost.

Again, whilst there is but this one allusion to cleansing in the epistle, a dozen may be counted which refer directly to the great Gospel gift of Pentecost.

In the next epistle pureness and purity are used in their generalized meaning, and therefore need not be considered, seeing there is no reference in them to the subject in hand.

However, we will notice the following—2 Cor. vii. 1: "Having therefore these promises, beloved, let us *cleanse* ourselves from all defilement of flesh and spirit, perfecting holiness in the fear of God." Evidently this passage might be rendered: "Let us keep ourselves from sin." But if this be objected to, still, we maintain, that it would be putting the words of the text to an enormous strain to make them teach a distinct second experience, after conversion.

In this epistle also are a dozen passages referring to the Pentecostal gift.

In Galatians, whilst there are thirteen passages bearing on the Pentecostal gift, there is not one concerning the blessing of purity.

In Ephesians, there is mentioned cleansing in connection with the whole church of God as follows, "That He might sanctify it, having cleansed it by the washing of water with the word, that He might present the church to Himself." But we simply quote it as sufficient for our present purpose, remarking that this solitary mention contrasts with twelve mentions of the gift of the Holy Ghost in the same epistle.

Passing over the intervening books, containing as they do seven mentions of the one and none of the other, we find the passage in Titus iii. verse 5, which will repay careful study in this connection, "Not by works in righteousness, which we did ourselves, but according to His mercy He saved us through the washing of regeneration and renewing of the Holy Ghost, which He poured out upon us richly."

Here cleansing is connected with the first stages of the Christian life, and the distinct Pentecostal experience is made to follow regeneration or cleansing.

But the modern interpretation makes washing to follow regeneration. Hence it is evident that this modern nomenclature does not closely follow scripture utterance.

In Hebrews ix. 14, is the following: "How much

more shall the blood of Christ, who through the Eternal Spirit offered Himself without blemish unto God, cleanse your conscience from dead works to serve the living God!" Now this is evidently a strong passage in favor of the teaching that our gospel provides for purity of conscience. But does it in any way imply that heart purity was to be the second blessing of the gospel? Does it not rather refer to the fact that the outcome of the gift of the Spirit, when retained, would secure a pure and holy life, by enabling the possessor, in place of trying the impossible task of regulating his life by laws, the prolific source of dead works, to serve the law of the Spirit, that is, the living God?

In 1 Peter i. 22: "Seeing ye have purified your souls in your obedience to the truth unto unfeigned love of the brethren," the work of purification is made to mean the same as keeping from sin through the appliances of the gospel.

But in the first chapter of John, 7th and 10th verses, are the great bulwarks of this nomenclature. And yet how carefully they have to be manipulated to have them do service here!

We maintain that if one is not hampered by the modern teaching concerning heart purity as the second blessing, he will infer at once that this is but an emphatic statement of the doctrine of conversion. For there is no hiatus between the two thoughts to admit all that is implied as preliminary to the second or cleansing blessing. The plain inference here is that every one who obtains forgiveness obtains cleansing. "If we confess our sins he is faithful and just to forgive us our sins, and to cleanse us from all unrighteousness." Plainly here cleansing is connected with confession of sins as forgiveness is.

Of course if the doctrine of heart purity, as the great distinguishing experience of the gospel, was established in a multitude of passages, then this curt allusion to the subject might be readily admitted as interpreted by the whole. But to build up such a massive structure on such a narrow basis is one of those strange efforts to be found no where outside of dogmatic theology.

In the Book of Revelation are a couple of instances where washing or cleansing is used, but they so clearly have reference to forgiveness of sins that we need not further weary the reader even by quoting them.

Such then are the *weighty* reasons offered us by many modern theologians why we should substitute the term *heart purity,* the *blessing of a clean heart*—being *cleansed from sin,* or similar expressions, for the plain emphatic teaching concerning the gift of the Holy Ghost, as the distinct blessing and glory of the present dispensation.

But further we ask the reader to contrast the indefinite character of the passages alluding to cleansing, with the clear-cut, distinctive teaching of those which refer to the Pentecostal gift.

"This He spake of the Spirit, which they that believed on Him were to receive, for the Spirit was not yet given because Jesus was not yet glorified."—Acts vii. 39.

"Behold I send forth the promise of my Father upon you; but tarry ye in the city until ye be clothed with power from on high."—Luke xxiv. 48.

"And they were all filled with the Holy Ghost."—Acts ii. 4.

"And ye shall receive the gift of the Holy Ghost."
—Acts ii. 38.

"He hath poured forth this which ye see and hear."
—Acts ii. 33.

"And the Spirit bade me go with them, making no distinction."—Acts xi. 12.

"And as I began to speak, the Holy Ghost fell upon them, even as on us at the beginning."—Acts xi. 15.

"It seemed good to the Holy Ghost and to us."—Acts xv. 28.

"And he said unto them, Did ye receive the Holy Ghost when ye believed?"—Acts xix. 2.

"The Holy Ghost which was given unto us."—Romans v. 5.

"If so be that the Spirit of God dwelleth in you."—Romans viii. 9.

"For the kingdom of God is not eating and drinking but righteousness and peace and joy in the Holy Ghost."—Romans xiv. 17.

"But we received not the spirit of the world but the Spirit which is of God."—1 Cor. ii. 12.

"Now He that establisheth us with you in Christ and annointed us is God."—2 Cor. i. 21.

"Received ye the Spirit by the works of the law or by the hearing of faith?"—Gal. iii. 2.

"In whom having also believed, ye were sealed with the Holy Spirit of promise."—Eph. i. 13.

"If any fellowship of the Spirit."—Phil. ii. 1.

Contrast, we say, these few rendered extracts, taken from a multitude of similar ones, and the astonishment grows that any persons, with the Bible in their hands, would attempt the herculean task of substituting this grace or result of the Spirit's presence for the gift of the Spirit Himself.

Should we examine the expressions perfect love, entire sanctification, or any other terms after this method, we would find that their claims to be accepted as successful rivals of the Pentecostal gift would be quickly disposed of, as in no sense charged with the meaning ascribed to them.

And further, we assert that all lovers of the truth will arise from this close study of the subject with a sense of relief, the result of finding that the Bible is so clear and emphatic on the subject, and that it strips the whole Pentecostal truth of the mystic, inconsequential reasonings with which this modern departure from scripture nomenclature has enshrouded it, while Pentecost is seen to stand out sublime, robed and radiant with the clear light of unadulterated truth, the great fact of the ages, second only to its procuring cause, the death, resurrection and ascension of the Lord Jesus Christ.

But unlike the brightness of Sinai, which repelled, it attracts us to itself, till embraced in its mild glories, we, too, flame and coruscate with its splendors, and go forth in its power, witnesses for Jesus to His utmost power to save, and fulfil in us all the good pleasure of His goodness. Thanks be to God for His unspeakable gift.

CHAPTER XIX.

TEMPTATIONS.

OTHER SUBJECTS EXPLAINED THEREBY.—It is gratifying to know with what ease the seeming mysteries of many theological puzzles are made manifest, and their intricacies explained, when this great central truth of Pentecost is brought to bear upon them.

What multiplied difficulties have connected themselves with temptations when considered with the blessing of cleansing from inborn sin according to modern teaching.

In the teaching of many modern writers on this subject, it is affirmed that in the justified state temptations come from within and without, but that in the entirely sanctified they only come from without. As further explaining the matter, it is said that when Satan tempts a saint whose heart is pure he finds no response from within, but if only in a justified state, the tempter is co-operated with by traitors within the heart, who generally help him to make short work with his victim.

Now, as we have in other places remarked, this statement of doctrine is true to facts when it is properly interpreted, but the modern interpretation is both wrong and misleading. In its true explanation it points to the teaching of Paul where he discourses concerning the Spirit. He shows clearly and repeatedly that the only provision made for successfully resisting temptation is by following implicitly this one law.

When for this simple gospel provision we substitute the effort to do right from a sense of duty, to carry out the rules of the Bible as rules or laws of life, then Satan has immense vantage ground against us, and is constantly successful in plying us with temptations. His success, then, is like that of a warrior who, besides his besieging army, has part of his forces as traitors in the camp of the enemy; success is almost certain to crown his efforts.

Need we illustrate this truth? Select any form of right-doing along this legalistic line and see how speedily the statement is proved. Let it be that of keeping holy the Sabbath. Now after the most rigid observance of pious rules concerning its sanctity, at the close of any one Sabbath-day sit down and see if the conscience is perfectly clear and the record of the day perfectly satisfactory.

You read in the Bible that you must not think your own thoughts, speak your own words, nor do your own works. And this rigid rule, be it remarked, is in perfect harmony with New Testament teaching. Now apply these rules to your conduct. You point to the fact that you have stopped unnecessary household labors. But are you sure of this? Have no unnecessary fires been kindled? No unnecessary utensils been used, calling for additional labor in their cleansing? One additional piece of delf, polished for luxury or convenience sake, and not as a work of mercy or necessity, breaks the spirit of the law as certainly as the act of the Israelitish woman who was stoned by Moses for picking up some chips to light her fire.

Then as to the words spoken. Have none been uttered

at the table concerning what was on it, or concerning individuals whose names chanced to come up in conversation, but what were in perfect harmony with this law?

What about thoughts? One minute's thinking our own thoughts breaks the rule as certainly as hours spent that way.

Any one who examines the subject thus closely will find that in endeavoring to keep holy the Sabbath-day by the help of the laws of scripture, he is at a tremendous disadvantage, and his state is aptly described by a garrison trying to defend itself against open enemies and secret traitors lurking within the walls. Defeat under such circumstances is absolutely certain.

The same result would be arrived at in examining efforts to keep the laws of the Bible concerning "Always abounding in the work of the Lord," "Redeeming the time," or "Praying without ceasing." No matter how satisfactory the conversion has been, no matter how clear the testimony of the Spirit to sins forgiven or to entire sanctification, if efforts are made to obey these precepts as laws of holy living; if, in short, there is any attempt to walk by these rules in place of walking by the one rule of the New Testament, the law of the Spirit, certain failure is courted, and he illustrates this state of temptation from within and without.

But when this figurative language is made to do duty for one who rejects this law of liberty both in theory and in practice, then its use is misleading and ruinous to Christian character. Those who reject this obedient walk in the Spirit are spoken of by the apostle as going about to establish their own righteousness, and not submitting to the righteousness of God.

Of course, most, if not all, of those whom we aim at will not accept this description of themselves as true; and yet we maintain that it aptly describes every Christian who rejects, in practice, the law of the Spirit as the one and only law of life; for thereby they reject the only way whereby the righteousness of the law, that is, the righteousness of God—being perfect, as our Father in heaven is perfect—can be fulfilled in them.

To bring out these thoughts still more clearly take an object lesson.

Here is a modernized testimony on this point: "Having received the blessing of a clean heart, I now find that my enemies are all on the outside. I have no temptations from within."

Now, in the multitude of cases which this testimony represents it is not used as figurative language, referring to the contrast between legality and spirituality, but has laid aside its figurative garb, and is supposed to be a positive fact, a testimony to the fact that now that the heart is pure, having been cleansed from all sin, there is really a radical change in the temptations with which one is assailed.

But submit this statement to closer scrutiny, and see how it will shrink from it. Can anyone define the two kinds of temptation thus indicated? Examine the temptations of Christ, and see if the mind can grasp a stronger form of temptation than they were. Satan took advantage of Christ's hunger to tempt Him. Of course, we all regard the hunger as not a temptation, but as simply an incident in His life, and yet an affliction or trial plainly ordained of God—"Then was Jesus led of the Spirit into the wilderness to be tempted of the devil."

Evidently the essence of the temptation was to break the fast without being perfectly true to the Holy Ghost. For if the Spirit who came upon Him at His baptism led Him to fast, He also must show Him when to end it. It was then a sufficient answer to give to the suggestion to turn the rock into bread, that when the time to fast appointed by the Father was ended something better than dry bread would be provided. And His words were prophetic, for at the close of the fast days, when the time appointed of the Father came, as revealed by the Spirit, then angels ministered to Him a richer repast as to variety than that hinted at by Satan.

Now let any one who has been called of the Spirit to fast, examine his experiences and see if the essence of all temptation in connection with hunger is not concerning his taking into his own hands to end it without waiting for the distinct sanction of the Spirit.

Moreover, he will have to confess to himself that such temptations act upon the innermost part of his being; temptations which shake him to the very foundations of his belief in God. What if he made a mistake in thinking the Spirit led Him to this fast? What if He should get no release from this conflict? What if exhausted nature should, in the end, have to resort to the stone-made bread, that is, take food within reach, but without divine sanction as clearly given as that which led to commencing the fast? Would not failure in the one case make the other a mere fancy of the brain? And would not that undermine the whole superstructure of supernatural religion? For the call of the Spirit which led to commencing the fast, we will suppose, was as clear as the knowledge of sins forgiven.

He who has passed through such an ordeal of temptation can appreciate the words, "tempted in all points like as we are." But of whom but Christ can it be said, "yet without sin." Alas! how have we, through the very sorrows of failure, learned to triumph, learned how to be tempted without sin!

How much easier the form of temptation which attends a self-appointed or periodic fast! For then, as the time appointed is a fixed quantity in the mind of the one fasting, all he has to do concerning hunger is to fight it after the Dr. Tanner style, knowing that when the clock points to a certain hour food can be taken with even keener relish than before.

Is it possible to place temptation connected with such a fast beside the temptation of Christ? Why, after the forty days were passed, even then there was no certainty that the fast was ended. It was only then that hunger was realized, but no knowledge was yet given that the divinely appointed fast was over.

We repeat it, that the very essence of Christ's temptation was the fight of faith that the Holy Ghost who descended upon Him at His baptism was leading Him in the strange vicissitudes of this lengthened fast in the wilderness, and, unlike Dr. Tanner, He had no set time ahead of Him, which, if He should reach, would necessarily end His hunger.

Those who have entered into Christ's temptation by experience cannot but realize that the nomenclature concerning within and without in no wise adequately defines temptation as known in their experience, unless the words are transposed, making Christ's temptations represent *the within and without* kind, and those connected with periodic fasting represent *the without* type.

Look, for a moment, at the second temptation of Christ, and it tells us the same story.

The way of the Spirit is ever too slow for headlong, impetuous humanity, hence, when once we become sure that we are anointed of the Holy Ghost for the accomplishment of any definite work, temptations meet us at every turn to hasten matters beyond the apparently slow but sure guidance of the Spirit. Has not God set us apart to this work? Are we not immortal till our work is done? Hasten on, then. Why take the laboriously slow way of descending by human steps? Launch into the air, the Divine must be invoked for speedier success.

Now the essence of the temptation is to still have steady faith in our divine call, and yet calmly wait His way, to abide by God's methods, even amidst the taunts of zealous workers, who, like Christ's brethren, say, " If thou doest these things show thyself unto the world."

Here, again, those who, having received the Spirit, essay to walk in Him, and those only can enter by experience into the fierce nature of these fiery trials that try all those who persist in striving to live the Christ life. They, too, know how tame beside such soul trials are the temptations along the legalistic line of Christian work.

But the temptation of all temptations comes when, after fully realizing that we are possessed of real spiritual power, and yet that from the highest to the lowest, whether in the church or out, all who are not thus spiritual are likely to antagonise us; then it is that we can, like Christ, be tempted to use this power according to the rules of human prudence.

For we well know that if we yield in the slightest degree in this direction, not only will this antagonism cease, but more immediate results might be witnessed. Hence the subtle temptation to abandon the unpopular way of the Spirit, or mix with it ways more popular, at least with *good* people.

"All these things will I give Thee if Thou wilt fall down and worship me," is not then a silly nursery story of a personal, visible devil, asking us to bend our knees to him; but is a subtle, apparently reasonable thing, backed by the testimony and example of the majority of professed Christians.

To those who successfully withstand these well circumstanced temptations, we again repeat, the nomenclature concerning the within and without has no meaning, only as it points to the difference between the fight of faith along the line of obedience to the Holy Ghost as the one and only law of spiritual life, and the unsuccessful effort to *live* a holy life by the observance of rules and regulations, intermingled with trust in Christ for pardon and cleansing.

But what, it may be asked, is the origin of this nomenclature? Well, we maintain that in every genuine case of sanctification there is a beginning in the Spirit, and as with the Galatians, a running well for a season. Now, during that season, whether long or short, they are led directly by the Spirit, and so fulfil the righteousness of the law. The contrast with the former experience is great; and the within and without nomenclature is readily adopted, just because it indicates a contrast.

Now, no sensible harm results from its use under these circumstances. But when, like the Galatians, after having begun in the Spirit, they begin the effort to be made perfect in the flesh; that is, turn away from the law of the Spirit to any extent, to laws and regulations as rules for holy living; then it is that the danger element comes in, and the within and without theory becomes a species of transcendentalism, whereby some forms of sin are sublimed into infirmities; mistakes and sins, which, in place of being frankly confessed that they may be forgiven and their stain cleansed away by the blood of Christ, are presumed to be covered up in some mysterious way by the atonement, and they are accounted holy in spite of the existence of sin in their lives. Thus, by this human device, God is made the minister of sin, and the very atonement a hot-bed of semi-Antinomianism.

Are these terms Scriptural? We certainly think they are not—that they have no Bible warrant whatever. For we have failed thus far to find a passage containing these words, or similar ones in connection with the word temptation.

But we do find many portions of God's Word which make against the theory in a marked degree.

Here is one: "In all points tempted like as we are, yet without sin." Now, according to this theory, Christ could only be tempted from without, that is, like one who was entirely sanctified, and hence, as an example of successfully resisting temptation, he is confined to the few who, during the Christian era, have belonged to this class. To all others His temptations could be in no wise helpful.

If this is true, is it not strange that Paul, one of the most careful of writers, should have failed to mention it, and not seem, by this expression, to include all who were tempted.

Again, in this connection, we would remark that the clause, *without sin*, would be still more misleading, presuming this theory to be true; for the entirely sanctified soul that successfully endured temptation, would not need this limiting clause in the comparison, for he, too, in this case, would be tempted without sin.

So we see that, by this theory, Paul would not only narrow down to a few persons the example of Christ's temptations, but would further restrict them by the words, "yet without sin," to the instances where the entirely sanctified yield to temptation—a veritable case of *reductio ad absurdum*.

Take another example. James declares, in the fourteenth verse of his epistle, that "each man is tempted when he is drawn away by his own lust and enticed."

We ask anyone to try and fit this within and without theory to these words. *Every man* here must include the entirely sanctified, or the verse would not be true. Hence, James proclaims it as a fact, that the entirely sanctified, when tempted, " is drawn away by *his own* lust and enticed." Can anyone imagine a more *within* kingdom than lust?

The unrenewed man may feel the pressure of poverty, and desire to have wealth, but when tempted through that desire to steal, he may either resist or yield to that sin. If he resists the well-circumstanced temptation to purloin a sum of money, he is as guiltless of that sin as would be an entirely sanctified man in the same surroundings. If he takes the money, he sins just after the pattern of Adam's sin.

Thus the closer we look into the matter the more evident it becomes that it is a hopeless effort to classify temptations on the basis of the without and within theory. Every man is tempted alike, *everyone*, including not only the entirely sanctified, but Christ Himself; the only difference between Christ and every other man, including Adam, is that He only lived a life from beginning to end without once yielding to temptation, that is without sin.

Still another passage reads, "There hath no temptation taken you but such as is common to man." 1 Cor. x. 13. Here Paul was writing to Christians, and he maintains that no temptation meeting them was different from those common to all men. Is it possible to discover the without and within theory in this verse? Verily, we think not. For if there is any part of our being, however cleansed and purified, that cannot be reached by the tempter, then there are some temptations that are not common to all men.

Therefore, we contend most seriously that this without and within theory, with the meaning which most modern writers give to it, is unscriptural in language, and is untrue to facts, and, therefore, should be discriminated against—both in testimony and teaching.

CHAPTER XX.

MISTAKES AND INFIRMITIES.

LET us now turn the brightness of Pentecost upon these hitherto undefinable subjects and see if we will not be gratified with the result.

First, stay a moment to note the chaotic state into which these and kindred questions have fallen.

There are mistakes—and mistakes, that is, there are two distinct classes of them. That this is absolutely certain, a very little consideration of the subject will show.

A man makes an error in adding a column of figures, but by a cross-count he easily corrects his mistake and the incident has no after-consequences either as regards his material or spiritual welfare.

But another man makes the great mistake of his life by failing, at some supreme crisis of fate, to accept salvation, and all his after-history, whether in time or eternity, is cursed through that mistake.

How absurd to class these two incidents as of the same kind. And yet custom will sanction the word mistake as appropriate for both.

Take now these two incidental illustrations as indicating the two extreme meanings of the word mistake and try to find the dividing line between them, and see how difficult the task. Are all mistakes in figures excusable? and is every neglect of spiritual advice culpable? Who has ever had the courage to draw the line of demarcation here, or secured the admiration of the ages in so doing! Do innocency and guilt shake hands across this line, or is it a great gulf, fixed and impassable?

Scientists have striven in vain to draw the line of demarcation in nature between animals and plants, or between plants and minerals, although the extremes in all three realms are pronounced in their differences, and yet we believe that the latter task would be easier than the former.

True it is that many attempts in the religious world are being made to accomplish this impossible feat, attempts which only make the darkness which covers it more visible.

Take up almost any of the modern treatises on holiness and see with what a confident air the author approaches this subject, and then notice the few generalized remarks with which it is gladly dismissed.

Notice also how this subject is manipulated so as to be the scapegoat of any defects in the creed of the author. We refer here especially to those authors who make their *personal* experience the great sun and centre of their system of ethics and cause all things therein to revolve around it.

For all defects in that system or personal experience are flung into the great waste-basket of Antinomianism —the atonement—and by labelling them mistakes and infirmities, are supposed to be got rid of in some mysterious way which will not bear too close inspection.

Let us attempt to generalize the many systems of this

kind which dot the theological firmament, thus. When the sinner is convicted for sin and comes to Christ by faith, all his former sins are cancelled and he is made a child of God and an heir of Heaven. But sin—inborn, original sin is not blotted out, and so it is necessary that this be cleansed away by a second application of the blood of the atonement. Now he is fully equipped for running the Christian race. But upon the review of any given section of his Christian life he will see many defects in it requiring confession and the re-application of the cleansing fountain. These defects are called mistakes, infirmities, or errors of judgment, and are supposed to be overlooked or carried away by the cleansing blood continually or fitfully applied.

Now question critically this weak part of the creed and see how unsatisfactory the answers will be. Will these mistakes or infirmities be cleansed away if they are not confessed? If so, why confess them? It must then be a work of supererogation to do so, seeing the one who does not is fully as well provided for as the other. If it is replied that this confession and faith is necessary for the continued application of the cleansing blood, then it is manifest that the confession must be *continual* to correspond to the need. If not continual, but fitful, then it is in order to give the number of times per day or per year that this duty must be performed to secure satisfactory results. But no one has ever formulated this rule, hence, as usual, the questioning process leads to an acknowledged uncertainty.

Again, take the instances where there has been a *conscious* mistake, or error of judgment, and before the duty of confession concerning it is performed, it is in order to pronounce upon it as to whether it belongs to the class of sins which needs to be repented of, or simply to the class of infirmities which only needs to be confessed. But where is the rule by which to discriminate here? It must be admitted there is none, and so as before the result is utter uncertainty.

And so, in either case, the best that can be done along these lines is to avoid looking too minutely into the subject, and content oneself by ever and anon going through the *form* of general confession of sins of omission and commission, re-consecration, and acceptance of forgiveness and cleansing.

We are aware that many a Christian who has given substantially this experience by word of mouth or at the point of his pen, will be startled at its appearance when thus put in cold, matter-of-fact shape, and be inclined to disown it; for the unction which always hitherto accompanied it tended to cover up its defects. Nevertheless, it will not require much effort to find out that we have correctly portrayed the vast majority of holiness experiences of the present day.

But, as before intimated, we have simply reproduced these experiences here, to show how unsatisfactory the whole subject of mistakes has been left by the modern formulators of holiness creeds.

But all these mists and uncertainties are cleared away when the Holy Spirit is welcomed to the believer's heart as the one and only law of his life, for then, whatever the outward expression of his life as viewed by others, whether certain acts are called mistakes, infirmities, or sins, when judged according to the narrow creeds of the legalist, he knows that through them all he is so guided that his acts are worthy of His Divine guide, that is, he walks worthy of God unto all pleasing.

But, exclaims one, is this *Gordian knot* cut by simply calling wrong right? By no means, but by always and in all places doing right, and never walking in uncertainty concerning anything.

He that doubteth, that is, is uncertain concerning such a trivial matter as eating, Paul reasoned, was condemned. How much more concerning many things which are smuggled in amongst mistakes and infirmities by many a sincere professor of holiness!

So the only way out of the infinite difficulties connected with the mistake question is and must be some rule whereby we may walk worthy of God unto all pleasing, even amidst the mistakes and blunders, real or apparent, which constitute the woof if not the warp of our finite lives.

But this whole subject of mistakes and infirmities which so troubles the legalist is so thoroughly, so completely disposed of by accepting and walking in the Spirit, that it at once sinks down to an unimportant matter, to be dealt with rather as a subject for speculation or curiosity, than as one of vital importance.

However, before entering into the realm of speculation concerning it, we delay a moment to remark that he who teaches a creed concerning holiness containing in it a place for mistakes and infirmities needing from time to time confession, forgiveness and cleansing, should hesitate to call it a creed concerning *holy living*, seeing no provision is made in it for such living.

For if a believer has lived a holy life during the past year will not his confessions, his re-consecrations and his being re-cleansed imply dissatisfaction with his life and put him in the anomalous place of being harder to please than his Master? For as he has walked worthy of God unto all pleasing during the entire year, the act of confession pronounces on the verdict of God as faulty and refuses to accept it as final.

Now the only way out of this absurd attitude of the soul towards its Maker is the admission that the believer has not lived a holy life during the time in question. But, again, this inevitable conclusion takes its revenge on the creed and proves to a demonstration that the profession of holiness along the line of this creed does not mean that the believer bears witness to *living* a holy life, but only to an *effort* in that direction.

From all of which the crushing conclusion is arrived at, that any professor of holiness who makes provision in his creed for mistakes as a proper cause for confession, consecration and cleansing, thereby vitiates his profession of holiness before all men, and renders his creed, as a holiness creed, a misnomer.

Certainly we are not, in all this, ignoring the fact that plenteous provision is made in the Gospel for forgiveness and cleansing as often as the believer, having fallen into sin, complies with the conditions of the Kingdom of Grace. What we are emphasizing is the patent fact that this is not the holy estate which the scriptures describe as normal to him who walks in the Spirit, that is, it is not Bible holiness.

And now a few words concerning mistakes, to satisfy

the legitimate curiosity or speculative tendency of the thoughtful reader.

There are different shades of meaning to this word, and it is well to know which one we adopt when we assert that the fully saved do or do not make mistakes.

There is a sense in which freedom from mistakes would mean absolute perfection, even the perfection of God. But in this sense no act of a man is free from mistakes, for all he does of necessity has the finite clinging to it. Man is an imperfect because a developing being, and therefore nothing connected with him in thought, word, or deed is absolutely perfect—that is, free from mistake. Hence all men, including the fully saved, are not only liable to but are always making mistakes—that is, thinking, speaking and acting in a way which comes short of absolute perfection.

Again, the word mistake takes to itself a relative meaning when an action is compared with an ideal lower than absolute perfection, and yet as high as the finite can reach in thought or has seen in reality.

For example, take the life of John Wesley, either in its entirety, or any part of it, and we have no difficulty in forming a more perfect ideal compared with which his life was full of mistakes. He might have preached a few more sermons, he might have travelled a few more miles; in short, he might have crowded into his wonderfully active life a few more activities which would have left his life still more complete than it is—that is, with a few less mistakes.

Again, one may take the life of John Wesley and compare his own life with it, and discover defects or mistakes as compared with it, and so admit that, in comparison with such a model, he is not free from mistakes.

Still, again, every mistake committed by us may, for aught we know, propagate itself throughout our after life as a continuous defect or source of weakness. For example, a child is dilatory during his school life, and his consequent defective knowledge will tinge his whole after career, and render it necessarily defective as compared with what it might have been, that is, full of mistakes.

Now, in all these meanings of the word mistake saint and sinner are alike involved, and the old Latin proverb, "*Humanum est errare*"—it is human to err—is correct when applied to every son and daughter of Adam.

Every person who is not a fit subject for the asylum readily subscribes to all these truisms concerning mistakes, and it seems like mere child's play to draw the attention of our readers to them. And yet there are not wanting those who seem to think that when we talk or write concerning having the witness of the Holy Spirit,

> "That all we do is right,
> According to God's will and word,
> Well pleasing in His sight,"

that we are assuming to be free from mistakes according to one or all of the meanings of the word above alluded to.

But there is a Bible sense in which the fully saved do not make mistakes. Take any point of our life, and it must be possible for us to live the best possible life, all things considered, thereafter, and this life would certainly be freed from mistakes when compared with that best possible life.

God must certainly have in His mind concerning every one of us a life which, starting from any moment, may be perfect, complete, holy, unblamable in love, entire, wanting nothing—in short, well pleasing in His sight; and to say that such a life is full of mistakes is a confusion of terms, if not of ideas.

Now God has made provision for every one of us to live this best possible life, and every one who abides in Christ, is indwelt by the Holy Ghost, and by Him guided into all truth, must live this very life, else he cannot be walking worthy of God unto all pleasing—he cannot be fully saved.

CHAPTER XXI.

PRAYER AND SCRIPTURE STUDY.

JESUS CHRIST illustrated in His life, as well as taught, the inherent antagonism between that which was spiritual and that which is legalistic. He in His own individuality represented the mind of God, and called upon all lovers of the truth, that is, all who were ready and willing to hear and obey the voice of God as Abraham and Moses did, to come to Him as representing that voice.

As a matter of history, the Abrahams of His time did recognize the voice of God in the call of Jesus, and forsook all and followed Him.

But the legalistic, that is, they who had permitted worldly aims and desires to weaken and destroy this inward voice, refused, and the inevitable result was that sooner or later they antagonized Him.

Jesus interpreted the universal thought of the heart of man when He declared that "the kingdom of God is within you," meaning by this *within kingdom* the innate knowledge possessed by every man that God can speak to him, and that it is wisdom and safety to obey that voice above all others.

Now we all know that had the multitude, headed as they were by the Scribes and Pharisees, investigated honestly the claims of Christ, they would have found them genuine, and would have become His glad, obedient followers.

But they loved the praise of men more than the praise of God, that is, although to follow this inward kingdom promised them ease of conscience and future blessedness, nevertheless, because the immediate prospect was that of deprivation as to temporal blessings, they decided against Him.

Christ made His appeal to man in his individual, not his corporate capacity. Hence each individual soul was called on to decide alone for God, with the knowledge that possibly, yea, almost certainly, he would be deciding against the masses, and so it meant literally to forsake all to follow Him.

What wonder, then, knowing what we do of the tendencies of human nature, that only the few followed Him and the many rejected Him.

But of those who refused to cultivate the *kingdom within*, various classes existed then as they do now. However, we will divide them into but two classes for our present purpose, viz., those who quenched the light within them and openly and as a matter of course accepted the world in its place, and those who undertook to make a compromise.

Now these classes cannot be known by simply naming them Scribes and Pharisees on the one hand and the multitude on the other, for both the laity and the priesthood furnished examples of lovers of the truth—men who became obedient to the faith.

The class of compromisers was composed of those who had a certain respect for this inward light, and to meet its claims for attention had become religious. They had listened to any teaching which promised them satisfaction concerning this thing. Hence to them religious observances were means to an end, and that end was to satisfy this inward want, this craving after soul rest.

The real compromise entered into was in accepting outward religious observances and listening to their voice with punctilious exactness rather than to the direct voice of God.

The advantages connected with this course were, that they could still retain the praises of men and all worldly advantages and avoid the pains and penalties connected with a spiritual life. True, they were required to pay no small price as their part of the contract. This price consisted in self-mortification, rigid observance of many rules and ceremonies and in alms-giving.

Here, then, you have the legalist of the days of Christ, and of all ages. Then the outward expression of his life was that portrayed by Christ—making long prayers, fasting twice a week, giving tithes of all his possessions, and minute observance of the Mosaic laws, with multiplied Rabbinical additions.

But did he obtain the soul rest after which he sought? By no means. For when John the Baptist came preaching repentance they gathered about him, hoping that he could supply their felt lack. But so soon as they found out that he appealed to that within kingdom, and demanded unqualified obedience to the voice of God, and did not countenance compromise, they speedily turned from him.

Again, when Jesus appeared they flocked about Him,

evincing by this very act their conscious lack. But, yet again, when they found out that He appealed to their conscious knowledge of God, and demanded implicit obedience to the reigning sovereign of the kingdom within them, even when the possibilities might be the loss of all worldly goods and of life itself, when, especially, He poured contempt on all their compromising acts of worship, not even excepting their careful observance of Sabbath laws, they rejected the kingdom of God against themselves, and turned against Him in persecuting hate.

The mass of worldlings treated the claims of Jesus with indifference, too much occupied with their eager pursuits to take time even to persecute Him. But the legalists of His day had no other alternative. They must either give up their religion or prove Him an impostor, seeing He had pronounced on their compromising efforts as vain and foolish.

They, in their opposition to Jesus, were really defending their religious practices. For if Christ was right, then, manifestly, they were wrong.

No issue ever was more distinct and clear, and therefore when they would not trust to the light that was in them, seeing they had the suspicion it would lead them to Christ, and the loss of all else, they must, perforce, do their utmost to show that He was wrong, that is, they must antagonize Him.

Now this will be seen to be the true explanation of the conflict which has been in the world since the days of Cain between legalism and spiritualism. It still exists although under different forms, and will exist while the world lasts.

The Holy Ghost, the sent of the Father and of the Son, has to-day taken the place of Christ, and appeals to this within kingdom, offering Himself to voice the mind of God to the soul of man under all circumstances and for all time.

But He, like Christ, makes His demands as an absolute sovereign, requiring instant, uncompromising obedience in every direction. No plea of fearfulness concerning the way He *may* lead, as to its being seemingly difficult, or requiring the loss of *all* things, can be for one moment allowed. He asks for full right of way throughout the entire being, and refuses to do His work when any conditions whatever are put upon Him.

Now absolute abandonment to the claims of the Holy Ghost, after this practical method, is as full of pains and penalties to-day as ever it was, and hence the temptation to compromise is as strong as when Jesus met it in His day.

Need we say that this compromise is witnessed in all efforts to meet the claims of the conscience by multiplied religious rules and pious observances, when the Holy Spirit is practically ignored as guide into all truth.

It matters not if these rules are directly or indirectly sanctioned by the Bible, still the essence of legalism must be there if the one practising them does not fully admit the claims of the Spirit, and act out his faith in those claims in life.

And moreover as the Godhead presses those claims of the Holy One for full, practical recognition either by providence or living testimony the legalist either surrenders or desires to surrender to His righteous demands, or tends more and more to assume the attitude of antagonism.

This thought is the true explanation of Christ's universal law, interpreted by Paul in the words "All that will live godly in Christ Jesus shall suffer persecution." There is war, perpetual war between the carnal and the spiritual—between him that walks after the flesh and him that walks after the Spirit—and will be to the end.

In the present time the compromise which is attempted is to substitute for the guidance of the Spirit rules or laws concerning prayer and scripture study. We use these as representative experiences.

Now there is nothing intrinsically bad in either. Who would presume to pronounce anything but commendation on the act of devotion or earnest perusal of the Bible? Nor would any one be justified in placing limits here as to time, place or quantity. Like acts of beneficence, in themselves they compel admiration. But it is just because they are of the essence of good that the legalist, who either through ignorance or wilfulness, fails to give the Spirit right of way in his being, turns to these, and multiplies his rules and regulations about them, and then, by listening continually to the exacting claims of these *rivals* of the Holy Ghost, strives to make up for what is lacking in his being through his failure to walk in the Spirit.

It matters not then whether once, twice, thrice or more times per day he essays to have seasons for prayer and reading, or whether one, two, three or more hours per day be the regulation time for those devotional exercises, the spirit of legalism must ever be present, and the danger of becoming pronounced in antagonism to the claims of the Spirit grows apace.

Now if at any time when the legalist hears the call of the Spirit to give these entirely into His hands, with unlimited confidence that the outcome will be the best possible both for time and eternity, he can either heed that call, or disobey.

Peter, when called to go to the home of Cornelius was legalistic in the extreme, but evidently there was no injury either to him or others from this fact up to that time, for he had not been called to see the necessity of parting company with his early taught ritualistic practices, nay, the gift of the Holy Ghost had thus far tended to make him if anything still more punctilious in his observance of them. Hence his surprised reply to the divine request to "slay and eat," as it came to him in the vision from God, "Not so, Lord; for I have never eaten any thing that is common and unclean."

Now Peter might have still clung to his legalistic practices, and refused to let the Holy Spirit guide him in this thing, when he would have gradually or at once have ceased to be led of the Spirit, and another would have had to be found to take his place as the foremost man in the new dispensation.

But he was loyal to the Holy Spirit as having supreme right of way before all laws and religious observances however founded on scripture teaching, and therefore he flung these all aside and went to Cornelius *nothing doubting*.

At the present day the Holy Spirit retains supreme right to come between the professed followers of Christ and all rules and regulations concerning prayer, scripture study or any other religious observances, and he who questions His claim in this matter cannot walk in the Spirit.

It is true that he may pile up arguments in favor of the rules in question mountains high. He may show that they are not only founded on the traditions of the fathers, but upon the best commentaries of the scriptures, and that very many eminent saints grew still more saintly in the use of these identical rules for holy living. All this and more he may truthfully say, and yet, we repeat, that if through these reasonings, and even added fears of lawlessness or fanaticism, he refuses to recognize the absolute right of the Spirit to control his conduct after a pattern diametrically opposed to them, and show a readiness to act out this his faith in life, he fails to be led of the Spirit in this thing, and runs great risk of antagonizing Him ever after.

From all of which it is readily seen that prayer, scripture study, fasting, alms-giving and other works of beneficence are in themselves good things, and there is in them no necessary antagonism to the Spirit's work. And moreover it is quite possible for the professed followers of Christ to have rules and regulations concerning the practice of all these things, that is, be legalistic in practice and still be spiritual; that is, led of the Spirit, even as was Peter and the early disciples up to the time of the call of the Gentiles.

But it is not possible to retain spiritual life, and refuse to be led by the Spirit when He claims His right to come between any or all these legalistic acts and the soul, as guide supreme.

When choice is made as between these rival claimants for supreme right of way in the soul, then we either follow the Sp'rit implicitly and become or remain spiritual, or we turn from Him and become or remain legalistic as a compromise, the outcome of which latter course is certain to be antagonism to Him and to all who are spiritual, that is, led of the Spirit.

It will be in order here to compare the two ways which branch off in opposite directions from this point. To the one who forsakes the way of the Spirit for the ways of legalism comes no complete satisfaction in the practice of legalistic services. Take the effort to satisfy conscience in the matter of prayer. Take if you please the very best example of this class, one who not only prays frequently and for lengthened periods of time, but who also adds much fasting therewith, and see if the results are satisfactory. Will he not readily admit at the close of any year of such punctilious observance of his rigid rules concerning prayer and fasting, that he might have spent still more hours in the closet of prayer with advantage to his own growth in grace and the spiritual welfare of others? And, moreover, will he not confess that the performance of his acts of devotion was not always as intense and as free from wandering thoughts and other defects as it should be, and that therefore in this thing he cannot claim the well done of the Master, having the witness of the Spirit as to his having walked worthy of God unto all pleasing?

But the result in this instance clearly proves the impossibility of satisfactory results in any case when the way of Spirit is departed from; for by the deeds of the law, that is, in this connection, by following set rules and regulations concerning prayer and scripture study, no flesh can be justified, cannot so carry out the law as to be justified in the deed.

But there are not wanting witnesses to testify that success is the outcome of the way of the Spirit, and therefore we claim that with the distinct, unqualified promise that He, the Holy Ghost, will guide into all truth concerning both prayer and scripture study, substantiated by both apostolic and modern living witnesses to the result as being satisfactory and free from failure, that the law of the Spirit is the God-appointed way and the only way whereby the believer in Christ can regulate successfully times and seasons for prayer, scripture study and other devotional acts.

Of course the question will often be asked in the future, as it has been in the past, What will be the result of such a course as to these times and seasons? And as often the answer must be that no man can know beforehand such things. As God has made every one an individual, so both reason and the Bible intimate that He, the Holy Spirit, will deal with him as such, and therefore the experience of no two will be necessarily alike in this or any other matter. This knowledge, therefore, can only come to the individual as an experience and through experience.

But can it ever happen that a Christian will be led of the Spirit to discard times and seasons for prayer or Bible reading altogether, or for definite periods of time? Certainly, if it should be the best for all concerned, not otherwise. But assuredly he who can not trust the Holy

Spirit absolutely with this matter will never know the mind of God concerning this thing as a personal experience, for this barrier of unbelief, that is, want of confidence in Him must forever block up the way.

It is more than possible, it is highly probable that the exile of Patmos had no set times for Bible study during the period of his stay on that lonely isle. The early Christians had no New Testament to read, and the Old Testament was difficult of access, and absolutely out of the reach of most, and yet modern Christians often sigh for the return of these very times.

Again, many Christians have been so placed that stated seasons for private prayer have been an impossibility, when for lengthened periods of time it was impracticable to obey literally the command of Christ, "When thou prayest enter into thine inner chamber, and having shut thy door, pray." Now in all these circumstances of disability to attend to set times and seasons God has control of the situation, and therefore to that extent is responsible for the failure to read or pray after the manner of set rules. Would it be a greater reproach on God if the Holy Spirit, without the compelling force of providential circumstances, should guide a believer to lay aside his set rules for prayer or scripture study, or make any change however startling?

How narrow and contracted the conception of Divine guidance which would ever and anon bring the Almighty Spirit as a prisoner before the bar of reason to be tried by saintly lives, the traditions of the fathers or finite views of scripture teaching!

But have not some gone astray just here, and imagined

that they were led of the Spirit when time has proved that they were sadly astray? Certainly this has been a matter of history, and history will doubtless repeat itself again and again in this thing.

We may question the wisdom of God in entrusting such grand possibilities for good to man when many will use them to their most serious damage; but then an intelligent view of the case will make it necessary also to question the wisdom of the Almighty in committing to his creature man such things as the grain producing grasses, with all their possibilities of food and luxury, when he can and does turn these very blessings into a curse by passing them through the still.

No doubt the Allwise God, He who seeth the end from the beginning, took in all such possibilities of use and abuse when He committed the gospel in all its fulness to man, and ordained it as a fundamental law of the kingdom of grace, that all spiritual provisions, when brought near to man, should prove either a blessing or a curse, should be either life unto life or death unto death to all who came within their divine influence. This is God's law in nature, why should we show surprise if it obtains in the realm of grace?

CHAPTER XXII.

THE LAW OF THE SPIRIT AND THE DRESS QUESTION.

WHILST we have seen in the foregoing chapters the hand of God in providing a certain rule of faith amidst all the perplexing questions of the soul in its inner life, we shall none the less admire His wisdom in providing the same ultimate law for regulating the external acts of a religious life.

Apart from this rule, what inextricable confusion prevails in the religious world concerning the simple matter of dress, for example! What able pens have been employed in discussions concerning what was ornamentation in dress and what was not, concerning the character of gold in this connection as to whether it changed its nature when composing ring, watch-guard or time-piece! What denunciations from the pulpit and pen against the products of the air or field when transferred to a lady's bonnet! And, again, what ability exercised in their defence! And yet after the expenditure of such mighty efforts, how meagre the results as to any uniformity in teaching or practice concerning what dress best becomes the profession of godliness.

True it is, that the narrow sectary will often point to a few of his church who have adopted some kind of sameness in attire, and claim that

> "These are the Temple of the Lord,
> And Heathens all beside."

But one has to be the rankest of bigots not to know that Heaven is of vastly greater dimensions than such contracted thoughts would permit it to be.

However, apart from such dogmatic teaching, there is much perplexity amongst sincere, conscientious believers concerning this thing.

Now these difficulties cannot be classed correctly after the loose pattern of extreme apostles of the dress question, who, with one sweep of the hands, divide all into two and only two classes, viz., those who, in obedience to their notion of Bible law, dress in plain clothes, and those who will not submit to such unadorned apparel because they are not willing to obey God.

With many the conflict is really concerning submitting to be governed by the dogmatic teaching of others, without being convinced in mind as to what is ultimate truth in this connection.

Very many are puzzled beyond expression concerning Paul's law of expediency: "All things are lawful for me, but all things are not expedient." What is expedient and suitable to the spiritual interests of others in connection with their dress is to them a perplexing, because an unsolved, problem.

From personal experience and observation, extending through many years, we are inclined to believe that no one subject requires the regulating hand of Divine guidance more than this troublesome one of dress, and on this account we deem it wise to devote a chapter to its full consideration.

Now, as contrasted to the many rules and regulations concerning this matter which have been laid down by men, some of them not wanting in scholarship and Christian graces, the teachings of Christ require each and every one of His followers to be taught personally by the Holy Spirit as to what is right in his or her case. And ample provision is made for all in their individual capacity to learn, not once for all, but day by day, just as required, what is the proper practice for them. And so it comes to pass that all may know continually just how to act and what to do concerning this thing with unerring certainty.

The law of liberty in Christ Jesus, *i. e.*, the law of the Spirit, makes free from the law of sin and death, from all the dogmatic teachings of individuals or combinations of men.

It is then the privilege of any child of God to learn from the Spirit direct just what to wear and what not. But it is not possible for one to teach another ultimate truth concerning this thing.

If these two thoughts are followed to their legitimate results, the great beauty and harmony of God's arrangements can best be witnessed. For if one may not dictate to another concerning this thing, then censorious judging one another is ruled out, and each one must leave his brother to stand or fall to his own master.

And if provision is made for each one in his own right to obtain clear instructions concerning dress, evidently, there is no need for the intervention of any other ultimate teacher of truth in this direction. ."And all thy children shall be taught of the Lord ; and great shall be the peace of thy children."—Isaiah liv. 13.

Did not the prophetic eye of the writer of this passage take in this possible rest from clashing views and dogmatic teachings when the work of the Spirit should be fully and generally recognized? What a change would come into the spirit of modern Christianity if the peace-procuring reign of the Holy Ghost were fully recognized!

But the dogmatist is ever ready to spring to the front with his pet subject and denounce all who do not dress according to his notions, on the assertion that they are *scriptural* and, therefore, obligatory on all. He quotes the one or two passages which seem to sanction his extreme and narrow views, and then maintains that for a person to say that the Spirit taught him or her to dress different from his teaching, would be the same as saying that the Holy Spirit led him to disobey plain Bible commands.

Of course, if this reasoning of the dogmatist is without a flaw, the conclusion is inevitable, for God cannot contradict Himself. That is, in this connection, He cannot have given a universal command against wearing gold or ornamentation of any kind as applicable to every son and daughter of Adam, and then relax this law in favor of any one individual. To admit this possibility would at once undermine all confidence in the character of God and throw doubt on all Bible teaching.

Besides, it would weaken and circumscribe the deliverances of Jesus concerning the Holy Spirit as Guide into *all* truth, if He found it necessary to hedge about the Spirit's work with rules concerning such an important matter as dress, and forbid Him to act the part of teacher concerning this thing.

Now this apparent incongruity will naturally prompt us to intelligently investigate the whole question from the scriptural standpoint, to see if it is the manifest intention of the Bible to lay down minute laws by which we should regulate our personal attire.

Naturally, if this work of guidance concerning dress has not been committed to the Holy Spirit, as the words of Jesus plainly indicate, then we shall look for a clear, unmistakable statement of the fact; and moreover we shall expect to find such carefully prepared rules and directions for dress as would rival the advantages of a personal supervision and direction such as Christ described the Spirit's guidance would be.

Now, after carefully studying the Bible with reference to this question in all its bearings, we give the result of our researches in the following two propositions or canons, viz.:

1. The Scriptures nowhere give forth a *particular* deliverance on this subject of dress, suitable to all times.

2. That the graces of the Spirit are the only characteristics by which the followers of Christ are to be known, and that any style of dress so conspicuous for its gaudiness or plainness that real spiritual followers of Christ could be singled out from others by it, is contrary to the spirit of the teachings of the Bible.

The two and only references which seem to imply a *particular* deliverance on this subject need to be examined here.

The two passages are 1st Timothy, 2nd chapter, 9th and 10th verses: "In like manner, that women adorn themselves in modest apparel, with shamefacedness and sobriety; not with braided hair, and gold, or pearls, or costly raiment;" and 1st Peter, 3rd chapter, and 3rd verse: "Whose adorning let it not be that outward adorning of plaiting the hair, and of wearing jewels of gold, or of putting on apparel."

First, suffer us to give some of the inferences drawn from these verses.

It is pretty generally taught that the writers of these paragraphs were laying down laws to be observed minutely by all Christians during all times.

That these passages condemn the use of gold or pearls as ornamentation in any form, and that any part of one's apparel which is superfluous, and hence only for adorning the person, is absolutely forbidden.

Most writers and teachers on the subject of holiness, we freely admit, accept these two canons as fairly embraced in the teaching of these verses. Hitherto there has been considerable unanimity in the published and spoken views of professors of holiness on this question.

But when it comes to practice there is infinite variety witnessed. One section condemns the wearing of gold, even in a watch or marriage ring. Another will pass these, but draw the line rigidly on wearing chains and earrings. Some rule out all unnecessary tucks and flounces in a dress pattern, and are horrified at the very mention of flowers or plumes, others admit the flounces and tucks, but wax eloquent against flowers and plumes. Many are troubled in conscience about plaiting the hair, but do not hesitate to substitute rolls, bangs, or frizzing. Then as to costly array, opinions as to what is costly array are simply too numerous to mention.

Smile not, dear reader, for we are dealing with facts —facts of vital importance in the eyes of very many good people. If all the time spent in anxious thought and prayer concerning the details of this question had been spent in attacking Satan's kingdom under the guidance of the Holy Spirit, the god of this world would have been driven from many a stronghold he now occupies.

And after all, who has reached a satisfactory conclusion in practice when adopting these rules to start from? The business man, on Sunday morning, doffs his blue jean suit, not to don another clean suit of the same material, but to put on a broadcloth coat, and goes to church a well dressed man, so much so that a prince at court in the days of the apostles might well envy him, and yet the extremest of the extreme apostles of the dress question will not find fault with him because he has flung aside his common clothes, and *adorned* himself in more costly array.

And so of woman, she may throw aside her calico, or linsey-woolsey garments of home life, and adorn herself with silk or velvet for church, so long as she hoists the holiness banner of a hat without trimmings and a dress without golden brooch. Nay, she may throw up her *gloved* hands in pious horror over her neighbor who, although clad in calico, has a feather in her hat or a piece of gold in either ear.

Are we finding fault? No, we are simply dealing with facts, and showing that there is no uniform practice with those who accept this as the real, legitimate teaching of the apostles—are only emphasizing our contention that there cannot in the nature of the case be anything but confusion in the practices of those who try to draw particular teaching concerning the dress question from these passages. It is simply impossible to accept these rules and be consistent with them in practice. All who throw stones, that is, criticize others in their dress from the standpoint of these rules, live themselves in glass houses, and are liable any moment to have them shattered.

But it is argued the word gold is mentioned distinctly, and therefore it must be wrong to wear this metal. But we reply, this sharp literalism always overshoots the mark, and speedily brings about rare contradictions.

See how this rigid method of interpretation will make the apostle quickly contradict himself, for Peter tells us in the fifth and sixth verses, that "after this manner aforetime the holy women also, who hoped in God, adorned themselves, being in subjection to their own husbands: as Sarah obeyed Abraham, calling him lord."

If we look up the Old Testament history we find Abraham, when sending for a wife for his son Isaac, sending with Eliezer, his servant, presents of earrings and bracelets of gold. Now, there could scarcely be a safer inference than that Rebekah, and Sarah, whose name is particularly mentioned as one of the holy women of old who adorned themselves in a becoming manner, wore such ornaments. To take the opposite of this would compromise the character of Abraham.

What, for example, would be thought of the consistency of a professedly godly man, whose wife,—a professor of holiness, and one who had refrained from wearing gold on religious grounds, having recently gone to her heavenly home—he, now, whilst professing the utmost regard for the departed, honoring her memory in every public way, takes the first opportunity afforded of destroying her example, by going out of his way to purchase golden ornaments and present them, nay, have them put on a prospective daughter-in-law? And yet this would justly portray the character of Abraham, if Sarah, from principle, refused to wear golden ornaments. So we have to come to the conclusion that, if strict literalism must be accepted in interpreting this chapter, St. Peter first commands women under no circumstances to wear gold, and then tells them to imitate in their adorning a person who did wear gold.

We, therefore, reject these inferences or rules as not the correct interpretation of the scripture teaching on this subject, because as rules they are impracticable and make the writers contradict themselves.

Again, these rules do not harmonize with other parts of God's word. For example, the only dress which was made according to divine description, that for Aaron, had ornaments of gold and precious stones in it. It would be passing strange to have the Bible denounce the wearing of gold as wrong, and yet sanction it in a particular instance without noticing the apparent inconsistency, and giving the reasons for it.

At Mount Sinai, when the Israelites had sinned, God required them to take off their ornaments preparatory to punishment. But this was evidently a temporary matter, and only seemed to sanction the wearing of them under ordinary circumstances.

Our Saviour, discoursing on dress, drew attention to the lilies arrayed in beauty beyond the splendor of Solomon, to show how He would care for those who left the matter of dress in His hands. Did it ever strike the reader that the illustration would be strangely out of place if all ornamentation in dress was strictly forbidden?

We think we have thus shown that these passages from the epistles do not enunciate a particular rule or rules on the subject of dress, suitable to all times.

But may they not have been intended as of particular application to the churches to which they were sent?

Now if the writings of the apostles and prophets be closely examined, it will be seen that, as with other parts of the Bible, there is a general principle running through them all which is applicable to all Christians to the end of the world, whilst there are particular illustrations which were necessarily restricted to their times.

The general principle is, that the graces of the Spirit, Christ-likeness, are the true adornment of the Christian, whether male or female. By no ingenuity can the scriptures be made to contradict themselves here. On this sublime subject all parts of the Bible are eloquent and harmonious.

The prophets paint the beauties of salvation in richest colors, no imagery being thought too extravagant to typify the soul-beauties which are the heritage of God's people. Hence it is said: "He will *beautify* the meek with salvation." The apostle points to the Christian as being ' changed from *glory* to *glory* as by the Spirit of the Lord," and in the Apocalypse we have the vision of the Church " *adorned* as a bride for her husband," and this adornment, we are minutely informed, is represented by white robes, "which is the righteousness of saints."

And now come in these particulars by way of contrast. Let not the adornments of the body be so conspicuous as to divert attention from the graces of the Spirit. Naturally he seizes on conspicuous articles of attire for illustration—a gold ornament then represented a hundredfold its present value, a gold ring that a laboring man to-day could purchase for one day's wage, would cost then a hundred days' labor. If illustrations were now looked for in this connection it would scarcely be gold or pearls, seeing they are now so cheap.

It is a significant fact, in this connection, that St. Paul, when writing to Timothy, at Ephesus, directs him to regulate the tendency there to extravagance in dress, but when writing to Titus, in Crete, concerning the conduct of his converts there, whilst drawing particular attention to drinking wine and other matters, does not touch the subject of dress; showing that, whilst in the main dealing with general principles, he was also writing with special view to meet the different needs of the particular churches.

One instance of this particular teaching for localities and times is given in one of the following verses, 1st Timothy, 2nd chapter, and 12th verse: "But I permit not a woman to teach." Now, if St. Paul was laying down a rule here to be observed in these days, then most Christians to-day, and especially professors of holiness, are openly and knowingly disobedient to the rule, for now women *teach* in our Sabbath-schools, in our evangelistic services, in our pulpits, and through the press; woman has no disabilities as compared with man in the Churches of to-day in this respect. The time had not yet come for woman to take her proper place in the assemblies of Christians, the change would have been too violent, and therefore it was to be left for after years to bring it about. We do not hesitate to restrict this rule of St. Paul to his times; why should we be so anxious to exalt a passing illustration, suitable only to those times, and evidently intended for a narrow application, into a universal cast-iron rule?

The second canon or rule follows as a natural corollary from the foregoing. The whole aim of the apostles is, we maintain, to emphasize the grand truth that Christ-likeness is the only badge, or token, of true discipleship, and at the present time, in some places, it might be emphasized with equal, if not greater force, by contrasting ostentatious plainness of dress with the graces of the Spirit, and might read, "whose adorning let it not be that of conspicuous plainness of dress, and absence of all ornaments, but let it rather be the absence of everything contrary to the spirit of the Master."

All of which brings us to the natural conclusion that only when men and women dress in harmony with the station in life where God has placed them, when they preserve the golden mean of not being too dressy on the one hand, or distressingly plain on the other, when, in short, they dress so as to deserve the compliment that Dr. Johnson passed on a lady of his acquaintance: "She was dressed so becomingly that I could not remember how she was dressed," then, and only then, can the graces of the Spirit have the opportunity they should have to show to all around their surpassing beauties.

Then take the argument of expense, or extravagance. Often an ornament is a gift—a gift which could not be turned into money, or parted with without breaking the Bible command, "Be courteous," so that in many instances this argument would fail to apply.

Then, again, a very strong argument with many is their own personal experience. Some professors of holiness after a prolonged resistance have adopted extreme views and practices on this dress question, and testify to special spiritual blessings received thereby, and they assume that because they were blessed in thus acting, all who do likewise will receive additional spiritual power and blessing.

Once we were greatly exercised on the subject of tea as a beverage, and after a prolonged conflict gave it up. In answer to the prayer of faith all desire for tea or coffee was eliminated from us, and so for several years we did not use them in any form. To us this experience was a means of grace. We were taught through it the power and condescension of Christ, and, moreover it was used of Providence to cure us of a throat disease of many years' standing. Of course we were disposed at first to put on spiritual airs over our experiences and urge other lovers of the "cup that cheers but not inebriates" to imitate, that they might obtain like spiritual benefits. But upon close investigation we found that the reason why we were called to this self-denial was the fact, that during our college life we had been intemperate in our use of tea, having habitually made use of its stimulus to keep us awake at night, for the purpose of study, and so our experience rather showed the fact of intemperance and inordinate desire on our part. Hence it was rather a reproach than a source of self-congratulation.

So we think that many who have had special conflicts over the dress question followed with peculiar spiritual illumination, will have to confess to some twist in their nature, some special leaning to "vanity fair," which required special legislation in their behalf, and that the relation of their Christian experience on this subject, whilst it exalts the power and condescension of their Master, serves to humble themselves, and in no wise makes them patterns for universal imitation.

If this view of the subject more widely prevailed we would hear personal narratives concerning conflicts over liquor, tobacco, and the dress question less frequently *repeated* in Christian assemblies.

Now in thus frankly discussing this question we wish it distinctly understood that we are not entering a plea for extravagance in dress or in favor of adorning one's person, nor yet striving to put a ban on simplicity of apparel. Our only object is to help perplexed ones to leave themselves in the hands of the Blessed Teacher without reserve, so that He, and not professed teachers of ultimate truth, may be able to guide them into habits and practices which will enable them the better to adorn the gospel of Christ.

CHAPTER XXIII.

PHYSICAL MANIFESTATIONS.

IT will be in harmony with this part of the subject to devote a chapter to the consideration of some of the physical manifestations often witnessed in religious gatherings, that we may see that the work of the Spirit, rightly understood, will prove to be a check on extravagance on the one hand, and cold formalism on the other.

Now holiness is a spiritual matter. It is a life. It is the life of God in the soul, showing itself outwardly in a life of perfect obedience—walking in all the commandments and ordinances of God blamelessly.

"If a man love Me he will keep My words, and My Father will love him, and we will come unto him, and make our abode with him." This is the true description of the holy man as given by Jesus himself—a man indwelt by the Trinity, and living a life of perfect obedience. Nothing can be admitted as a substitute for these in the make-up of a truly sanctified life.

When, then, any one tells of physical or mental phenomena in connection with his Christian experience, they may excite our curiosity or even wonder; they may even excite our admiration concerning God's condescension in adapting Himself to the wants of His people, but it all ends there. The only essential thing concerning all these things is the fact of walking with

God in glad obedience. How it was brought about, or how perpetuated, as regards outward manifestations, is clearly non-essential.

We emphasize this thought for a purpose, for it is the failure to properly classify essentials and non-essentials concerning a holy life that works so much mischief in the ranks of professors of holiness.

Now the essential part in the transaction of becoming holy, is the reception of God into our being. The manner of receiving Him is plainly non-essential, and its relation, whilst it constitutes a large part of Christian experience, and gives interest to our religious gatherings —for as no two experiences are similar, the telling of how *we* entered into full salvation will always, amongst other things, afford the charm of variety—yet affords no room for boasting, for there is no scriptural warrant for placing one above another in this respect. Dreams, visions, prostrations, tears, awe, silence, all clamour in vain for precedence here. If the Bible commands us to shout aloud for joy, it also says, " Be still, and know that I am God." If one would exalt the gift of tongues, the apostle brings him to order by showing that it was simply a sign for the unsaved, and of less value than simple testimony.

But man is ever prone to undervalue the spiritual and over-estimate the temporal or external, hence one of the greatest of all dangers to spiritual religion is from this source.

How this tendency is indicated in our thoughts about Pentecost, in magnifying to undue importance the sound as of a rushing, mighty wind, the cloven tongues as of fire, and the gift of tongues, and keeping too much in back ground the only essential quality of that blessed experience, namely, the reception of the "Comforter, which is the Holy Ghost," into the life and being of the disciples, in all His glorious fulness, as a permanent indwelling guest!

All these sensible tokens of the promises fulfilled became a simple memory when the day of Pentecost was past, with the exception of the gift of tongues, and that St. Paul declared to be of small import; but the gift of the Holy Spirit remained to every faithful disciple as a constant conscious possession. They were all filled with the Holy Ghost, and remained so filled, even as Jesus had promised: "He will abide with you forever." Hence it is recorded of Peter and John, when before the council, that they were *full* of the Holy Ghost. When the multitude chose men to administer their charities, they were exhorted to choose men *filled* with the Holy Ghost. It is said of Stephen, he was "a man full of the Holy Ghost." This was the crowning blessing of the new covenant, the fulfilment of all prophecy, and its continuance in Pentecostal fulness is the pledge of promised blessing.

This should be looked upon as the simple, normal state of the true Christian—being filled constantly with the Spirit, even as the disciples were filled with the Holy Spirit in the first days of the Church's history. This is the purchased possession for all Christ's followers. The Father is ever waiting to bestow it upon all for the simple asking, and the only condition to believers is present faith.

Oh! if Christians would but cease their cavillings and

reasonings about it, and, as little children, simply receive the Holy Ghost, and thus *know* of His wondrous power to bless, and make us a blessing, how would the church become glorious all within, and to Satan's kingdom would become terrible as an army with banners!

Satan well understands this, and hence concentrates his attacks against this experience. One of his chief methods is to induce Christians to substitute in their thought and teaching physical manifestations for the fulness of the Spirit.

We were once present at a holiness gathering where the following incident occurred. The public meeting was over, but a large number remained of their own accord in the church, for further waiting upon God. Pretty soon three persons, at short intervals from one another, fell prostrate on the floor, more or less in that rigid state familiar to those who have had much experience in revival work.

Then a young man, who was apparently acquainted with them, delivered a fiery exhortation to the forty or fifty people there, intimating that the blessing of entire santification was one thing, but that the baptism of power, of which this was an exhibition, was quite another matter, and he urged all present to look for this identical thing at once.

We noticed that nearly all present followed his instructions, and commenced to strain after like physical manifestation, as though it would secure for them some wonderful blessing.

Well, no one else managed to get into this psychological state, although the effort on the part of many was intense and prolonged; and although they were helped by one of the prostrate ones, who presently came to, and delivered an excited exhortation on the subject, using himself as an illustration of the baptism of power when thus received.

Now many would be inclined to pass by such an incident with a smile, and try to think no more of it. But that, we maintain, is not the part of wisdom. This incident is but one of a great many. Trace it back in its history and it is seen to have its origin in the prominence given by good and great men to physical manifestations in their work—that meeting being called the best or most powerful where *such* "demonstrations of the mighty power of God," as they were called, have been witnessed.

Now this subtle method of fostering a desire after strange physical and mental phenomena, by calling those meetings the best where they occur, cannot but bear such fruit as the above incident. There could have been none of this on the day of Pentecost, for it is said that they *all* spake with tongues—none of them lay around like corpses—all were able and ready to speak to the people who gathered around them of the wonderful works of God.

But the great error, productive of untold mischief, is substituting, either in part or whole, these things for the indwelling Spirit, the promised Comforter. Any admixture here, even in thought or in desire, is fraught with most serious consequences. The holy oil of the old dispensation, emblematic of the *promise of the Father*, was not to be tampered with, either by adulterating it or by imitating it, under the severest penalties; so, under the present dispensation, all imitations or admixtures with the "unction from the Holy One," secures the saddest results.

But not only is the phenomenon above mentioned often substituted for the Pentecostal gift of the Spirit, but other things are in part, if not wholly, made to represent it,—such as raising the voice to a high pitch either in song, in testimony, in prayer, or in shouting; and many services are considered to be eminently Pentecostal largely because of such noise.

And be it remembered, that at such times there are peculiar facilities for making mistakes in this respect; for there is ever a species of exhilaration connected with such use of the voice, as also from sympathetic communion with others in a like state of mental and physical activity, which can, and often is, taken for the real spiritual exaltation which is the result of the reception of the abiding Comforter. Hence the absolute necessity of guarding the sacred unction with a godly jealousy.

The only safe course is the scriptural one: to maintain most persistently that all these things count absolutely nothing in this connection; that they always have been, and forever will be, outside and separate from the scriptural reception of the Holy Ghost.

One of the evidences of the human origin of such imitations is the desire for their repetition. Being human in their source, they are necessarily ephemeral; as time goes on the original intensity diminishes—thins out—and then there is a call for fresh baptisms, repeated physical manifestations.

This is the prolific mother of many modern inventions

to bring about the desired results. Hence the exhortation to get down and call mightily for a baptism. Persons who but a short time before testified to the reception of the Holy Ghost as an abiding guest, will now pray most lustily that He, the Holy One, may descend down upon them, thus destroying their former testimony as to His continued presence in His fulness with them.

The fact is, it is a proof that their former testimony was not correct. They evidently are not acquainted with Him as "the promise of the Father," but have mistaken something else for *the* Pentecostal gift of the Holy Ghost. That something which they are struggling for can be repeated, and hence they labor on until often many are captured in Satan's net, and are deluded into imagining they have had a baptism because of pleasant sensations from the use of their lungs, or the awe connected with some strange manifestations on the part of a few who are affected by the unnatural strain upon their nervous systems.

We presume our words seem strong, and perhaps they take a tinge of indignation to them as we are reminded of the personal harm received from this very thing which we combat. How we have been enticed to accept these things for what our being craved! How we have been cheated out of our blood-bought privilege for many years of our religious life by these counterfeits! The glorious gift of God has been made to appear repulsive by human devices, and Satan used them to keep us out of our heritage.

And he is at his old devices yet. In this present revival of holiness these counterfeits are being more and more industriously put forward, not only to capture sincere seeking souls, but also to alarm and perplex those who have welcomed the Comforter into their hearts.

And yet if men would but take their Bible in their hands, and *try the spirits* by the written word, their true character would soon be made manifest. Christ is the true type of a Christian. For John says: "As He is, even so are we in this world."

Imagine the Saviour the centre of what some of those setters forth of strange doctrines call a modern Pentecost, where all are exhorted to pray long and loud, and agonize for a baptism, and then beside it put Christ preaching the sermon on the mount, and afterwards add "He shall not strive nor cry aloud, neither shall any one hear His voice in the streets."

True, some may point to the hosannas of the multitude when He rode in triumph into the city. Well, there can be no objection to bursts of enthusiastic joy at times when His glorious presence is revealed to individuals or to multitudes; then it is perfectly in order to triumph in holy song, or shout aloud for joy. What we do oppose is the attempt to get up the hosannas to order, and substitute another joy for the joy Divine.

Again, close observation will show this spirit to be unlike Christ in its arrogance and unteachableness. It does not exhibit that meekness which in honor prefers one another. It is impatient of contradiction and of restraint. It hesitates not to despise dignities, and fails to be subject one to the other in love. It does not readily obey them that are over them, but is ever ready to usurp authority itself. Home duties and quiet acts of beneficence are looked upon as of secondary importance when they seem to clash with public work, and therefore have to give way, Scripture to the contrary notwithstanding. In short it is not the spirit of Christ. It may boast of conversions, of sanctifications and of baptisms in others; but these are not scriptural tests, and should not be admitted in deciding concerning its character. Its only test we repeat is Christ-likeness.

This spirit does not show its anxiety for harmony amongst Christ's professed followers, by going to those whom they denounce as wrong, and inviting mutual conference, prayer, and waiting on God with careful, united study of His word, if by any means unity in the Spirit might be reached; but jumps to the conclusion that all who do not walk with them are opposed to *the* truth, and must be opposed and fought both publicly and privately to the bitter end.

There is no difficulty in judging righteous judgment concerning this thing if we follow scripture rules; but if we look for signs and wonders there will be enough of them to capture the unwary.

But it is not the positive evils resulting from substituting physical manifestations for the fulness of the Spirit that we deprecate most. The indirect evils resulting therefrom are still greater. The way of the Spirit is evil spoken of as these extravagances are witnessed, and thus a widespread prejudice is created, not only against the counterfeits, but against the thing counterfeited.

When good men lend their name and influence to promulgate the doctrine that the Holy Ghost manifests

Himself to His people most readily and most preciously where these physical manifestations most abound, it cannot but tend to awaken prejudice in the minds of many sincere Christian hearts. This we know from sad experience.

But with gladness that words cannot portray we can proclaim the Gospel news that the Comforter Divine is ready to come in Pentecostal fulness to every believer who will open up his being for His incoming.

Whether walking by the way, communing in the secret place of prayer, musing upon your bed, or gathered in the assembly of disciples, He is just now ready to enter in and dwell in all His radiant fulness.

Then so glorious will be His manifestations, and so wondrous the sense of completeness in Christ, so intimate will be your communings with Him, that to utter a prayer for a baptism of the Holy Ghost would at once shock your sense of propriety and appear but an insult to your ever-present, ever-abiding Guest and Friend.

If at any time you find yourself sighing for another baptism of the Spirit, be sure you have sinned Him out of His habitation, when the only way to recover the lost treasure is by the way of repentance and faith, not by human device. When genuine repentance, including confession of sin and perfect faith in Christ, are seen, then, and not till then, will He return to His own. All other methods lead to a counterfeit joy, which may feed the fires of fanaticism, but can never secure the peace unutterable and joy unspeakable, which are constantly ours when we are filled with all the fulness of God.

CHAPTER XXIV.

DIVINE GUIDANCE AND THE CARE OF THE BODY.

ALL parts of the Bible contain promises with reference to the welfare of the body. The Old Testament is very pronounced in its teachings that the welfare of the body was closely connected with a righteous life, and the New Testament likewise emphasizes this teaching.

Now this general truth is nowhere disputed. That "godliness is profitable for all things, having promise of the life which now is and of that which is to come" is an accepted truth to all who receive the Bible as a divine revelation.

Our Saviour is clear and authoritative in His statement concerning this thing, maintaining that the union between the two is so essentially close that he who properly attends to the first may dismiss all trouble concerning the other; "Seek ye first the kingdom of God and His righteousness and all these things shall be added unto you" brings out this thought in decided form. The best care of the body in all respects, according to the plain teaching of Jesus, is secured in seeking His kingdom and righteousness.

But it is evident that the mere attitude of seeking will not meet the case. Evidently it means that he only who seeks successfully these spiritual things secures the material blessings desired. But as in the previous chapters we have shown that the doctrine of Divine guidance is the major part of this kingdom, it follows that he who is led of the Spirit into all truth, and he only, secures all possible benefits for his body.

This argument would be sound and conclusive if there were no special allusions to this outcome of Divine guidance in the teachings of Christ and his followers. For the simple fact that the Holy Spirit undertakes to guide into *all* truth him who yields unreservedly to His leadership, must mean such knowledge imparted to him concerning the care of the body that when reduced to practice the result will be eminently satisfactory in all respects.

For the purpose of illustration imagine a community or nation or, for that matter, the entire population of the globe, in their individual capacity, yielding to the claims of the Holy Spirit as guide paramount, would it not follow that the best possible state of things would exist on this earth for securing the highest possible good for the bodies of all ?

The picture which here appeals to our imagination is attractive in the extreme, and it requires us to put a curb on our desire not to try our hand at descriptive details. But our present object is fully attained in keeping it before the mind of the reader sufficiently long to realize, in some crude form, what would be the advantages to the bodies of men should such a desirable condition obtain in our world.

Now whilst not all of these results can be look

when one individual walks in the Spirit in the midst of a crooked and perverse nation amongst whom he shines as a light, nevertheless, the best possible results must come to him which under the circumstances can exist. For if this proposition is not admitted then it would not be true that if all walked in the Spirit the best possible results for the body would be obtained by all.

It will then be seen, and readily admitted, that he who is led by the Holy Spirit, according to the promise of Christ, into all truth from any one moment of his life onward, from that moment on he is certain to secure the best possible care of his body in all respects, according to the judgment of Christ.

It is necessary to draw particular attention to the last clause of the foregoing sentence, "according to the judgment of Christ." For He only can take into His mind all the mighty interests which centre in any one of us, and adjust every fact in our lives so as to harmonize with all good temporal and eternal.

But do we know the mind of Christ concerning these things? Our reply is that we cannot know them any further than His own distinct utterances teach, and it is a legitimate study to gather these together as they have been recorded by apostle and evangelist for our edification and knowledge.

It will be found on close inspection that these statements of His are both few and generalized in their teaching. Nevertheless, whilst this is the case, they are very pronounced in showing that he who really enters into His kingdom and remains there will vastly improve his condition even as regards the body.

"Blessed are the meek, for they shall inherit the earth."—Matt. v. 5.

"Therefore I say, be not anxious for your life, what ye shall eat, or what ye shall drink; nor yet for your body, what ye shall put on. Is not the life more than food, and the body than the raiment? Behold the birds of the heaven, that they sow not, neither do they reap, nor gather into barns; and your Heavenly Father feedeth them. Are not ye of much more value than they? . . . And why are ye anxious concerning raiment? Consider the lilies of the field, how they grow; they toil not, neither do they spin; yet I say unto you, that even Solomon in all his glory was not arrayed like one of these. But if God so clothe the grass of the field, which to-day is, and to-morrow is cast into the oven, shall he not much more clothe you, O ye of little faith? Be not therefore anxious, saying, What shall we eat? or, What shall we drink? or, Wherewithal shall we be clothed? For after all these things do the Gentiles seek; for your Heavenly Father knoweth that ye have need of all these things. But seek ye first his kingdom, and his righteousness; and all these things shall be added unto you."
—Matt. v. 25.

"Jesus said, Verily I say unto you, there is no man that hath left house, or brethren, or sisters, or mother, or father, or children, or lands, for my sake, and for the gospel's sake, but he shall receive a hundred-fold now in this time, houses, and brethren, and sisters, and mother and children, and lands, with persecutions, and in the world to come eternal life."—Mark x. 30, 31.

Such is the unmistakeable teaching of Christ concerning the welfare of the body in the kingdom of Heaven. Now, if in this kingdom the law or guidance of the Spirit has supreme right of way to the annulling or superseding of all other laws, then it follows that he who accepts this kingdom and really obeys this all comprehensive law must inherit all these things—yea, they must be fulfilled in his life.

This distinct teaching of Christ was brought out clearly by His immediate followers. Hence Paul could, on the strength of it, confidently say to all veritable believers, "For all things are yours; whether Paul, or Apollos, or Cephas, or the world, or life, or death, or things present, or things to come; all are yours."—1 Cor. iii. 22.

He then who as a believer in Christ accepts the Holy Ghost and walks in Him by the moment, must inherit all temporal as well as spiritual promises, must have all his temporal surroundings whether concerning food, raiment, home and health of body in that form which harmonizes with the promises of Christ, that is, they will be the best possible for him, God being the judge.

It is true that to the unspiritual this last clause is a disappointing one and in their estimation vitiates the whole. But to meet this very objection, which must come from the carnally minded, Jesus has been careful to prove that God fulfils these promises to individuals not grudgingly or disappointingly but according to His own ideas of beneficence, which are higher and fuller in blessing than ours.

Therefore it follows as an absolute certainty that he who fulfils all the conditions secures for himself as an individual the best possible care for his body in all respects But as we have already seen this is tantamount to saying that in the doctrine of *Divine guidance* is wrapped up all possible temporal blessing for the body as well as for the soul.

To particularize, he who is led of the Spirit will not walk in darkness, that is, doubtfulness concerning eating, drinking and raiment, concerning labor and rest, or concerning health or sickness.

What! says one, Will he always be able so to adjust his clothing as to avoid catching cold, to so select his food amidst the dishonest competition of the present day as to never be imposed on by vile adulterations? In short, will he be so infallibly led that he will always bear a charmed life amidst infectious diseases and the accidents of life?

Now what we ask do these and similar questions imply? Do they not assert that, in the judgment of God, every pain and every accident, in short every inconvenience or deprivation of fancied good is an unmixed evil, is that which if we could avoid it would make for our good both in time and eternity?

But if this teaching on the part of such questioners can be made good, then we hesitate not to affirm that Jesus, by His promises, has left Himself no option in these matters. Then it would be an impossibility for any man who walked worthy of God unto all pleasing to suffer any of these things. To have the promises fail in any direction would compromise the Promiser.

But we maintain that it is not left to the finite mind to decide these things, for only infinite understanding is equal to the task.

Paul, we have every reason to believe, was as clearly led of the Spirit to Rome when he lost his life by this act of obedience, as he was when he went to Corinth to found a successful church. Immunity from accident or inconvenience will not establish the fact of being led of the Spirit any more than exposure to them will establish the contrary. And he who has not in his faith got beyond the region of judging of the Spirit's work by the apparent results in these things, has not got where he may know of the truth of the doctrine by experience.

Unhesitatingly, then, we answer, that we cannot seize on any one individual and say that if such an one walks continually in the Spirit no disabilities as pertaining to his body or mind can ever befall him. But with the same confidence we can also say that, selecting any one individual, if from this moment he accepts and walks in the Spirit, there shall be no incident in his life which will not fully harmonize with the promises of Christ, his life will be the best possible in these respects, God being judge. To particularize, he shall always be in the right part of the world, shall have the best surroundings, and that health of body which is the best for him and all concerned, and of no other person or persons than those who so walk in the Spirit can this be true.

Now this is absolutely true of the believer who walks in the Spirit whether he, in the case of real or threatened sickness, uses one remedy or another, whether he employs the skilled services of one physician or another, or whether he discards all alike at the instance of the Spirit. Moreover, the truth is not affected should his recovery from illness be in slow response to the usual laws of his physical frame, aided or retarded as the case may be by so-called remedies, or be instantaneous in answer to the living touch of the Great Physician. For he has followed his guide absolutely, and so all the powers of the human and divine blending together, the outcome must be the best possible both for time and eternity.

But is not the presence of sickness in the body the evidence that sin in some form is present? By no means, if the patient is at the time a believer and walking in the Spirit, for if so, then the Holy One is a partaker of, or at least a party to that sin.

For we are supposing that the person in question has been and still is obedient, moment by moment, that is, continually, to the Holy Spirit, as the living law of his life. He then has been guided into this truth or sickness. And if it is sin, then indirectly if not directly God is the author of sin.

But, says another, it is the law of the kingdom of grace that there should be no sickness in true believers who have accepted Jesus as their healer. Then, we reply, if this is absolutely true, it is as absolutely true that the Holy Spirit must guide our friend so as not to be sick, or if sick when the Spirit is accepted truly as guide into all truth, then, it is certain that He will guide him at once out from his sickness. Can there be any flaw in this reasoning? Is it not self-evident?

But, we remark, if any one takes this as a truth, viz., necessary freedom from sickness, and makes it a condition in his surrender to and acceptance of the Holy Spirit, then we say it is impossible for him to receive

Divine guidance. For the Spirit is an absolute sovereign and cannot, in the nature of the case, be bound by any stipulations concerning health of the body or any other thing.

Hence we emphasize the law of this spiritual kingdom to be that of absolute abandonment to the Holy Spirit. Calvinism, Arminianism, or any other ism, either in part or as a whole—set rules concerning dress or devotional exercises, doctrines concerning health or divine healing, or any other conceivable matter cannot be brought into this kingdom to regulate or fetter the work of the Spirit. The very first step to be taken to know the mind of the Spirit, which is true wisdom, is that indicated by Paul where he declares that if any man would be wise " let him become a fool that he may be wise," meaning in this connection, let him admit at the start that he knows nothing as ultimate truth concerning any or all of these things. Then it is that he may, nay, will become wise in any and every direction that that knowledge or wisdom shall make for his good.

But in order that the sincere seeker after truth may the better approach this mighty subject unfettered by prejudiced thought concerning what is the teaching of the Bible concerning sickness, it will be well to examine here the modern doctrine concerning it, which places sickness side by side with sin, and calls upon believers to accept salvation from it in the same way that they accept salvation from sin.

Now as when examining the Scriptures concerning rules for dress our only object was to clear away obstructions to full-orbed Divine guidance, so, in this case, we will examine this modern dogma from the standpoint of scripture in no spirit of hostility or antagonism to the *Divine healing* movement.

Moreover we contend that as those who hold and teach extreme views on the dress question, taking all their Christian work together, are proving themselves a great blessing both to the church and the world, so the apostles of divine healing, both by their godly lives and their intense Christian work, are a source under God of great benediction to others, and we hesitate not to give our unqualified God-speed to them and their work as a whole even when they cannot return like Christian courtesies.

In taking up the scriptural argument in connection with this important subject, in order to show that the Bible does not teach that the healing of the body is on the same basis as healing of the soul, and that just as all may come to God through the atonement made by Christ, and claim pardon and cleansing, so all can claim freedom from all sickness by simple faith. We contend that we do not need such a rule, even presuming it to be true.

On the day of Pentecost Peter promised to the multitude of penitents, that so soon as they accepted Christ by faith they were eligible to the reception of the Holy Ghost, even as they had received Him. Now Christ had described Him in one of His offices as guide into all truth, and this included guidance as to when we might use the prayer of faith for sickness.

Again, we remark, that in all fairness to this doctrine of physical healing for all it should rest upon passages in the New Testament somewhat analogous to those which teach the forgiveness of sins, both as to number and clearness of teaching.

We are prepared for the statement that the healing of the body is not as important as the healing of the soul, but admitting that, still our reasonable demand is for a fair proportion of such passages.

Now let anyone take up the epistle to the Romans, for example, and try to count the passages wherein the forgiveness of sin for all men is taught, and see how numerous they are. Why, the letter is full of them, until you are led to conclude that the whole epistle is one elaborate argument to establish the doctrine of forgiveness and cleansing from sin for all men.

Now continue your researches through all Paul's epistles and you find that they constitute but different changes rung out boldly and clearly on these doctrines.

But mark, you will not find one passage which either positively or by implication teaches this presumed doctrine of healing for all. But you will find several passages which it has taxed all the ingenuity of modern faith-cure teachers to explain away, lest they might seem to conflict with their teachings.

As for example, Paul's advice to Timothy, "Be no longer a drinker of water but use a little wine for thy stomach's sake and thine often infirmities." Any modern faith-cure apostle who would give such advice now to a Christian would be promptly ruled out of the circle as heterodox.

Again, where he discourses concerning his friend Trophimus, whom he left at Miletum sick, or Epaphroditus, who was sick nigh unto death, but who recovered, how opportune the circumstances to bring out clearly the modern doctrine of healing for all, but by no means can his language be made to give any aid or comfort to those who are striving to establish this dogma. Much less when he minutely describes his own bodily ailment, of which he did not recover at the time, but obtained the mind of God that it, the thorn in the flesh, was designed to remain for his spiritual benefit, can any supporting evidence be obtained from the whole account to strengthen the faith-cure extreme doctrine.

But note in the passing into what rare contradictions they fall in trying to explain away the whole matter. Paul calls this visitation an infirmity, and glories in it, as a blessing in disguise, saying, "Most gladly then will I glory in my infirmities." Our critics explain infirmities to mean something, anything else than a bodily ailment, for the only reason, as far as we can see, that it would destroy their doctrine if not so explained away.

And manifestly they are right, for if it was impaired eyesight, or any other bodily infirmity, then Paul would have to be accepted as an opponent to their doctrine, or as failing to live up to its privileges. Hence to a man they maintain that infirmities in this passage means something not included in the atonement. But the passage "Himself took our infirmities and bare our sicknesses," Matt. viii. 17, is often quoted by them as teaching that sickness and infirmities were atoned for by Christ, the same as sin, and they are thrown into confusion in the attempt to reconcile the different passages.

Some seem disposed to chisel out infirmities altogether from this sentence, and use only the word sicknesses as in the atonement. Others try to show that infirmities in the one place means quite a different thing from what it does in the other, and so make Paul culpably careless in the use of his expressions. From all of which we learn that if this modern dogma was accepted in the times of the apostles, Paul, judged by his writings, seemed to be ignorant of it, and even wrote as if teaching truths opposed to it.

Witness his statement that only a few were entrusted with gifts of healing. He did not teach that a few had the gift of healing for the maladies of the soul. That is, he taught that whilst the remedy for soul sickness was universal, that for the body was limited and confined to a few. "Have all the gifts of healing?"— 1 Cor. xii. 30.

Plainly, then, St. Paul cannot be brought forward as teaching clearly this modern dogma. Neither can John in his epistles be pressed into service here, for whilst there is much in them about forgiveness of sin, about the new birth, and freedom from sin, there is not one passage which has the remotest allusion to this subject. Clearly, then, if these modern teachers had to depend on John's letters to establish their doctrine they would find no help, and yet they are so full of teaching concerning forgiveness and cleansing that these doctrines could safely be left to stand or fall on his epistles alone.

The same may be said of Peter and Jude.

But in the epistle of James there is one solitary passage which seems, at first sight, to favor this doctrine. Now, granted all that is demanded by them concerning the teaching of this passage, is it not in order to doubt the claims of a doctrine, which has but one passage in all the epistles to rest upon, to be placed beside doctrines which rest upon a thousand passages?

But an intelligent examination of these verses will show that they not only do not teach the doctrine that sickness, like sin, is atoned for in the death of Christ, but they show quite the contrary. It is taught here that if the sick call in the elders, and they pray in faith over them, they will recover. There is no direction here for the sick to accept health like forgiveness through the merits of Christ, but their recovery is connected directly with the prayer of faith, as uttered by the elders.

Then James goes on to discourse on the power of prayer, and brings in as an example Elijah's prayer of faith by which the heavens were sealed up in the days of Ahab, so that no rain fell until he prayed again that the drought might end. Plainly, then, James connects the raising up of the sick by means of the prayer of faith, with such occasional miracles as scarcity and abundance of rain, when the result of believing prayer. But no one will have the hardihood to say that such things are in the atonement in the same way that the forgiveness of sin is. This passage, then, clearly places the recovery of the sick where it belongs, namely, amongst the extraordinary answers to the prayer of faith, and by no means teaches the general doctrine that all sick people, just as they may claim present forgiveness for all past sins by faith in Christ, can claim present freedom from all their sicknesses and infirmities by faith in Jesus.

The only argument drawn from the Acts of the Apostles is, that some of the early Christians, noticeably Peter, Paul and Stephen, healed very many, of their maladies. And yet Paul speaks of leaving Trophimus at Miletum sick, as if it was an ordinary occurrence, and makes no apology when recommending medicine to Timothy.

In the Gospels we have the narrative of Christ's miracles of healing minutely told. At different times it is definitely stated that He healed all that came to Him for healing, or even that had need of healing. But it would be a difficult task to connect healing of the body, even in the miracles of Christ with healing of the soul. True, in some cases He Himself did in some sense connect them, as when He forgave sin first, and then healed the body. But this was not always the case. For example, one person who was cured, when asked who performed the miracle, could not tell who it was. Again, when ten were cleansed of leprosy, Christ admitted that nine of them did not show even common gratitude for what they had received from Him.

Again, healing the sick was classed with other miracles which attested His divinity When He gave a commission to the seventy to pass through the land before Him as heralds, He gave them power to heal the sick, to raise the dead and cast out devils.

We call attention to the fact that healing the sick was not classed with the forgiveness of sin, but with raising the dead and casting out devils, things which were purely miraculous, and in no way depended on the faith of the parties concerned. They were to preach the Gospel and leave it for men to accept or reject it, according to their faith in Christ, but they were to positively heal the sick in the same way that they were to cast out devils and raise the dead.

There is nothing then in the Gospels to connect the

healing of the sick with the atonement, as sin is connected, excepting the one passage above quoted, and that, if it is pressed into service here, proves too much, for then it would make, as we have shown, St. Paul glory in his shame.

Many passages of the Old Testament are appealed to as teaching this dogma, but we do not deem it necessary to quote them and examine them one by one, even if we had space for such an exhaustive method of argumentation.

A few general thoughts will be sufficient to show the hopelessness of establishing such an important doctrine on these passages.

In the first place, the promises referred to had reference specially to the Israelites, and were connected with other national blessings promised to them as a peculiar people, if obedient.

Take for example that strongest passage in Exodus xxiii. 25, 26: "I will take sickness away from the midst of thee." In the first place, we contend that to secure the fulfilment of this promise it was necessary that the whole nation should walk in obedience to the commands of God. It can hardly be pressed into service for individuals who were obedient, when the nation as a whole had departed from God. If so, then the following promise also was certain of fulfilment: "The number of thy days I will fulfil." This would mean that no matter how sinful the whole nation, no matter how determined to persecute all who were faithful in their obedience, that every one who did so obey God was certain to live out the full number of days allotted to man, namely, three score and ten. Those who press this passage into service for establishing the extreme teaching of faith-cures must not shrink from this application of the text.

We hear that there are some who are beginning to teach that any professed Christian who dies before the age of seventy cannot enter heaven, and why should not this thought be encouraged if the first part is taken as literally true of every one who walks in the light of faith-cure teaching? For if one such should die before the above age, it might be correctly argued that, either he had failed in his obedience to God, or God had failed to fulfil His promise. And notice, that the Lord does not reserve to Himself the power to remove by accident. The faithful, obedient one, has a life insurance policy, good against all accidents, sickness, or the malevolence of man or devil up to the ripe age of seventy.

Now, to our mind, the only escape from these deductions is that these are promises of national blessings, and contingent on national righteousness. And we are inclined to think they were exclusive in their character, and confined to the favored Jewish nation. But, without pressing this thought, we maintain that when they are made to depend on that "righteousness which exalteth a nation," they are of little practical value in the present dispensation, and cannot be made to promise perfect health of body and certain old age to every child of Adam, irrespective of surroundings, just as the forgiveness of sin is promised to all.

Such general statements as those of David, when he says of God "who healeth all thy diseases," need not be discussed in this connection, seeing all accept the doctrine contained in them, and recognize the hand Divine in recovery from sickness, no matter what secondary remedies may be used.

And thus we have gone over the ground we intended, not perhaps with that minuteness of detail some expected, but sufficiently exhaustive for our purpose, which is not to disparage the faith-cure movement, but to do what we may to relieve it from the threatened inroad of legalism with all its evils. For while this method of presenting the whole subject guards against narrowness, and judging one another with censorious thoughts, it nevertheless secures all possible health to those who are prepared to come under the law of the Spirit in Christ Jesus, which makes us free from the law of sin and death.

These are the principal arguments which force upon us the honest conviction that, however plausible this teaching concerning healing of the body for all, just as forgiveness of sin is—it has no solid foundation in scripture teaching, and therefore ought to be rejected, whilst the use of the prayer of faith, in all instances where the Holy Spirit prompts its use, should be accepted as a glad privilege in the Gospel.

But, whilst unhesitatingly rejecting this peculiar modern tenet concerning sickness as having no firm basis in scripture teaching, we are profoundly convinced that, as a rule, health of body will characterize those who walk in the Spirit, and that instances of faith-cure, that is, where the prayer of faith at the instance of the Spirit shall raise the sick into health through the healing power of the great Physician will be multiplied, and at the same time those instances where will-power is evoked to a hopeless contest against the will of God will become less and less frequent.

CHAPTER XXV.

OBJECTIONS CONSIDERED.

IT is only reasonable to expect when a subject is brought to the fore which seems to demand a radical change in many directions both in doctrine and practice, that it will be closely scrutinized and objections urged against it from every conceivable direction. And it is not a good illustration of sound sense, to say nothing of Christianity, to treat these objections after a *special pleading* style. They should be formulated as nearly as possible from the standpoint of the objector and their full force admitted.

Truth, if it be foundational in its character, should show itself strong and all convincing after giving objectors the full benefit of every doubt.

We certainly propose to ourselves to so treat the objections here considered, and if we fail in so doing, or use the plausible arguments of mere theorists it will not be from design. So we court rather than shun the criticism of honest searchers for truth, and shall take it as a kindness when any flaws in our arguments or facts are pointed out to us.

For like the reader we have but one life to live here, and such vast interests centre in it that the desire to be right at any cost ought to be more than a sentiment.

It has been our way for many years to reduce every

thing to actual practice in life, and so, when we reply to objections, it will be understood that we not only reply by argument but from actual experience.

INFALLIBILITY—The first objection we will consider is the above for it generally first strikes the mind of the objector and seems to be the most formidable. It is urged that such teaching concerning Divine guidance virtually assumes that every one who accepts the Holy Spirit as guide into *all* truth, and acts out this profession in life is infallible. For, say the objectors, they claim that they are led every moment by an infallible guide, and hence their claim is tantamount to assuming that all they do, think or say must be absolutely right.

Now this objection rests *apparently* on good grounds, and cannot be passed by with a light remark or a denunciatory epithet.

But if the objector will examine his own mind he will find that the difficulty is there and not in the subject in hand. For he will find that he is taking some person, say himself, whilst not walking continually in the Spirit, and so fancies him suddenly claiming absolute perfection concerning what he knows from experience to be vacilating and faulty.

But why should it be so difficult to leave out from the consideration of this subject the actions and thoughts of one who is not led of the Spirit into all truth? If the objector will allow himself to conceive of a man really in harmony with the Spirit, and therefore walking worthy of God unto all pleasing, he would realize that no harm could come to the one so led, nor yet to any others through him, even if he did claim infallibility. For if he really does harmonize with God then all his acts, bearing on them the spirit and impress of the God of love, could in no wise militate against the best interests of all concerned.

But our objector may readily admit this and yet maintain that the real danger exists in persons who are not really led of the Spirit imagining they are and so becoming dictatorial, unteachable and in practice running into all forms of fanaticism.

Now that this is a real source of danger it must be admitted. Not only does the mind at once conceive of such possible danger, but such results have been actually witnessed in life. As a matter of history all those who have imagined they were led of the Spirit when they evidently were not, have not been confined to asylums.

When then this objection is pressed with the only object in view of regulating the subject of Divine guidance, it is in order. But when it is brought forward to prove, either openly or by implication, the impossibility or undesirability of Divine guidance then its origin as well as its use is evil and tends only to evil.

But we maintain that if such objectors consider the subject with sufficient care they will find that not only is there no danger in this direction, but that the thing they object to is the only effectual check upon the errors mentioned.

It is true that there is only one man who claims infallibility pure and simple, but the spirit of this dogma may be seen in every degree of intensity throughout the churches. What but this spirit can account for the fact that one professed Christian is so ready to denounce another because forsooth his shiboleth is mispronounced!

When Calvinist and Arminian leave calm argument for fierce denunciation. When an apostle of the dress question or faith-cure deals out anathemas on others who fail to interpret scripture after his thought, what is it but a faint copy of the Pope of Rome? Indeed, when professors of religion permit differences in creed, or sincere differences in opinion concerning what is *essential* truth to separate them in their Christian work, especially when each admits the Christian character of the other to harmonize with the Spirit of Christ, then, we maintain, we see a developement of this spirit of infallibility.

And strange to say this unamiable spirit is seen, often in its fiercest forms, in some of those who make the strongest claims to have the spirit of Christ. And yet why so strange, seeing Jesus Himself predicted that many whilst thus acting would think that they were really doing God service!

Now the doctrine of the guidance of the Spirit for every individual strikes at the very root of this, for it takes away the possibility of one dictating to another, or demanding the acceptance of his views of truth on the pain of his anathema. For, if the truth is fully recognized that every one must be taught directly of God, then no one will demand the acceptance of his views of truth as necessarily true for another. The utmost he can do is to commend his brother to their common Master to learn what may be ultimate truth for him.

It was thus that St. John was delivered from this spirit. For, after bringing to bear upon his readers his rich experience and knowledge of truth, he acknowledged that they had a source of knowledge superior to him, and after all his exhortations and teachings he reminded himself and them of this fact, saying, "The anointing which ye received of Him abideth in you, and ye need not that any one teach you." How utterly impossible for any man to dogmatize concerning truth, or to lord it over God's heritage if this teaching concerning guidance Divine for all is fully recognized!

Again it will be seen with what care this subject is guarded when it is understood that equal guidance for every individual makes it improper for one to attach undue importance to the "*thus saith the Lord*" of another. For if one with the possibilities of learning all needed truth for himself, directly from the fountain head of all truth, should accept as authoritative the teachings of another, however buttressed by claims to Divine inspiration concerning them, he would in that very act, sin against his own birthright, and put a slight on the Teacher Divine.

Hence it will be seen at a glance that the general acceptance of the doctrine of Divine guidance would reduce the evils resulting from false claims to personal guidance to their minimum, for they would in that case be confined to the one individual who had fallen into error.

And here we remark that the advantages of this Divine protection against the propagation of error can be best seen by contrast. For the loose, uncertain views held generally on this subject tend to make the multitude the lawful prey of any religious enthusiast who has the hardihood to declare that he has Divine sanction for his teachings. The effectual antidote for such poison has been too generally thrown away, and so it has come to pass that no teachings can be too extravagant to preclude the possibility of securing adherents.

But we further remark that the real objection to the dogma of infallibility is not aimed against the claim of being right in those things which begin and end with oneself, but against the claim made to regulate others. What Protestant would be troubled about the claims of infallibility on the part of the Roman Pontiff, if he did not demand their recognition by others when he undertook to regulate their consciences and acts? So if the doctrine of Divine guidance for every individual is confined to each in his relation to his Maker, and ceases to be Divine guidance the moment the effort is made to go beyond these bounds, and demand the acceptance of any deliverance as right because the outcome of Divine guidance, we maintain that even the word infallibility would lose all its terrors in such a connection.

But the word itself we contend is a misnomer when connected with any part of the subject. For the real essence of the word is that which speaks of the impossibility of being in error or of making mistake, with which definition the word plainly can only be applied to God Himself. For granted even that he who is led of the Spirit in any matter is absolutely right in that thing, yet this would not take away the possibility of one in such circumstances refusing to be so led, or even failing to be so led when he fancied he was. True, it is said in Isaiah that the "fool shall not err therein," but even this strong statement does not antagonize other Bible teachings which show that he may leave the way altogether, when to err would be a necessity of his state.

But do not some already claim to have illustrated Divine guidance for lengthened periods of time without one failure in being so led? Certainly. But it will be noticed from the foregoing how restricted the nature of this claim is. It is simply their witness to others that the relations between themselves and God have been the most satisfactory possible. But no demand because of this is made upon any, either to accept their teachings as correct or their acts as right. It is simply a testimony to a glad satisfactory experience, nothing more. Wherever it has been made to mean more than this it has been necessarily the outcome of evil.

There is no commercial value for instance in such a claim. If a man owes a debt, a *thus saith the Lord* from the debtor cannot affect the claim of the creditor before any tribunal earthly or Heavenly.

Nor yet can any personal revelation be successfully urged by one professing to be led of the Spirit as an apology for even apparent wrong doing.

We readily admit that it is possible for any one to be called on, like Peter and John in the early days of Christianity, to violate the laws of man. But even then provision, as we have shown, is made whereby those making the objectionable law can verify for themselves the correctness of their position, whilst, in the meantime, the ready submission of the law breaker to the penalty incurred, and the publicity of the transaction cannot but disarm or greatly weaken hostile criticism, and tend to annul the unrighteous law. But all such acts of apparent lawlessness, it will be seen, are not in the interests of private, personal advantage, but bear on them the mark of Christian benevolence, and so are easily separated from those acts which have their origin and centre in self.

But the objection may still be made that, indirectly, the wrong action of one who goes astray concerning Divine guidance affects others. If, for example, a wife and mother claims that she is led of the Spirit to forsake husband and children to attend to so called Christian work, in yielding to such an impression would not others suffer? Plainly this would be the case, and instances of this kind have come under our notice.

But we have also noticed that the greater part of the suffering was submitted to because of the prevailing superstitious reverence accorded to the claims of being led of the Spirit when made with great confidence. Now such a claim is either right or wrong. If it is right, provision is made in the gospel for all concerned to discover this fact, when it ought not to be difficult to adjust all things satisfactorily. But if it is not right, then what is it but a misfortune? And he who walks with God can best adapt himself to the serious affliction.

Is it possible for such a thing to be right? one asks. Well we have purposely used this extreme case so as to cover all the ground. But we entertain a very strong belief that Divine guidance reduced to general practice would make such incidents much rarer if it did not put them away altogether. For believing as we do that the general laws which unite families are of Divine origin, we would be surprised to see them deliberately set at naught by their Author. However, be this as it may, the point we make here is that in the event of diseases of the brain, which take the form of claims to Divine guidance in more or less startling forms, the safeguards thrown around this doctrine cannot but reduce the evils resulting from such sad afflictions to the least possible. So that when the whole subject is more fully understood and more generally realized in practical life, in place of seeing these sad calamities of life charged to spiritual truth, there will be the glad recognition of the Spirit's work as the great means of mitigating them. With what serene confidence, we add, can one who walks with God do his part under such circumstances, seeing he is not hindered, on the one hand by superstitious fear, nor on the other by dread of human denunciations.

DEPRECIATING THE BIBLE.—Another objection is that prominence given to Divine guidance tends to weaken the force of Scripture utterance as though it were not the sole rule of faith.

Our reply is that it tends to regulate, not to destroy this Bible authority. Certainly the Bible is the only authoritative revelation of God to man. But this Bible itself proclaims that its chief object is accomplished when it makes man acquainted with God, in the person of Christ, and with the Holy Ghost as the present representative of the Godhead on earth, that thereafter he may be led by the Spirit into all truth.

But it is urged by one objector that thus to constitute the Spirit supreme and ultimate teacher of and guide into all truth, would be attended with disastrous consequences. But we ask, Has the effort to make the Bible the sole guide in doctrine and practice been attended with satisfactory results? What doctrine, however monstrous, has not been professedly credited to Bible teaching? What practices, however they may outrage our innate sense of right, have not been claimed to be the outcome of minutely following scripture utterance?

Then, again, is not presumed Bible teaching made responsible for anathematizing and putting under pains and penalties those who are pronounced to be *heterodox?*

Also, in rejecting the Holy Spirit as the sole guide into truth ultimate and placing the Bible in His stead, do not the multiplied standards used in the church visible to-day proclaim the failure of this usurpation? If now it is asked, What is the teaching of the Bible concerning any one point? the answers are as various as the standards erected outside of the Bible. One refers you to general councils as giving Bible teaching with certainty, another points to some written creed, and still others to an individual—as Wesley, or Calvin, or Luther. Small wonder it is, that where such seeming anarchy prevails, many an individual should regard himself as the true interpreter of the Word, and deal out his mimic thunder in imitation of the former occupant of the Seven Hilled city.

Now we ask, is it not smile-provoking to hear one with such results before him, so manifestly the outcome of constituting the Bible the supreme guide for man, express fears concerning the outcome of again constituting the Holy Spirit guide supreme to every individual believer?

Moreover, it is a fact worthy of note, at this point of

the argument, that differences of opinion concerning the teaching of scripture are more rife and more intense, and their importance more exaggerated when spirituality is at its best under this regime. For example, the divisions amongst Methodists were most numerous and most pronounced when the average of spiritual life was the highest, and the same has been the history of every reformation in the Church since the early days when the Holy Spirit had right of way as guide supreme.

Now let it not for a moment be thought that we tax the Holy Bible with all or any of these things. What we do say is that men have taxed the Bible beyond its ability. They have attributed to it powers never conferred upon it by its Author. God the Father and God the Son ordained that the Scriptures should be searched to learn their testimony of God, and that the Holy Spirit should act as guide to individual man. It is the fact of turning away from the old paths that has wrought such confusion—a confusion that can only be avoided by a return to Heaven's appointed methods for Divine harmony.

Further, to show the utter hopelessness of arriving at unity in the Spirit by the methods that have thus far ended in such utter failure, we ask, let any candid, unprejudiced man read over Paul's argument concerning women taking part in religious services, and see if he dare say distinctly and without any circumlocution that the great apostle of the Gentiles did not distinctly teach that women should neither *teach* nor *speak* in Christian assemblies; and then, leaving Paul out of the question, let him read all other parts of the Bible bearing on this subject, and then see if he could have the hardihood to affirm that women have not scripture authorization to exercise these gifts as well as men.

Now it will at once be seen that we draw from this and similar conflicting thoughts in the Word, that if the Bible was originally charged with the mission which, since the days of Luther, has been ascribed to it, it is strangely furnished for its work; and however great would be the miracle which would bring about unity of faith without accepting its authority as supreme, it would require a still greater miracle to accomplish this result when so accepting its teaching.

Therefore, in view of all we have here said, and much more that might be said in the same direction, it must be evident that the objection concerning *disastrous consequences* cannot be a very strong one, and must be confined sooner or later to those who wish to lord it over God's heritage. These would-be Popes will ever antagonize the work of the Spirit, for well they know that every individual who fully accepts the Spirit to obey Him as the sole law of life is at once emancipated from their usurped authority: "for where the Spirit of the Lord is there is liberty."

But, persists one objector, have not incidents already occurred where individuals have testified, and that publicly, that they have been led of the Spirit to refrain from reading their Bibles, even for lengthened periods of time?

Well, suppose we admit this to be correct. Will it not be well first to ask if this has been the testimony of the many or of a few? If this has been simply an incident of experience in the lives of a few individuals, may it not be seen to harmonize with reason and common sense? For example, if a believer has for years made it a practice to read a large portion of the Bible every day without fully digesting that which was read, would it not be to his interest if a vacation of a few weeks or months were taken, not only to teach him not to exalt to undue importance his rules of Bible study, but also to afford the needed opportunity for thoughtful consideration? Now we openly proclaim that all the incidents, included in this objection, which have come under our personal observation, when carefully inquired into, could easily be accounted for after this philosophical, yes, common-sensed manner.

But certainly it is neither of the nature of philosophy nor sound sense to seize on a few rare incidents, and those out of harmony with the general experience of all, yes, and of the individuals themselves in whose lives they occurred, and found a valid objection thereon. We are satisfied that, in this case also, these objections will be relegated to those who shall have personal interests to serve in urging them—to those who make the mere reading of the Bible according to set rules a large part of their righteousness. From all of which it will be seen that the Holy Spirit, as guide to individual believers, may show Himself a foe to formalism or superstition in the use of the Bible without either depreciating or antagonizing that which is the outcome of His own heart.

And so, finally, we remark that our objector may see that close examination of his objection not only dissipates all fears in the direction named, but awakens the hope, nay, the belief, that the doctrine of Divine guidance is the great spiritual panacea for all the ills considered.

Not that we for a moment contend that the acceptance of this gospel remedy will bring all to think alike concerning all doctrines or practice. But we do believe that, whilst differences in opinion will still characterize different minds, there will be the full privilege to differ accorded by each man to his brother, and all persecution or denunciation for opinion's sake will be a thing of the past. "For they shall not hurt nor destroy in all my holy mountain, saith the Lord."

CHAPTER XXVI.

OBJECTIONS CONTINUED.

LAWLESSNESS.—Fears are entertained by some objectors that the acceptance absolutely of the guidance of the Spirit as the supreme law of life would tend to the despising of all lawful authority both in Church and State.

And here again incidents are not wanting in actual life to apparently confirm this thought, for it is true that some from time to time have set at naught all laws human and Divine under cover of this doctrine. This must be admitted frankly. And we further admit that it is the knowledge of such lawless acts on the part of some that surrounds the whole subject with real difficulties.

We well remember how formidable this objection appeared to us before we accepted without reserve the guidance of the Spirit. And we confess that, ere we gave up our fears sufficiently to abandon ourselves without reserve to all the consequences of this step, we were brought to the place where the terrible discipline of the past appealed as greatly to our fears of the future as any imagined results of possible fanaticism could do.

It is true we now smile at those fears, and unhesitatingly say, from the experience of several years, that they were all the time like Bunyan's chained lions. But we are assured that many are now as we were then—so placed that they do not see distinctly the chains. And therefore their objections appear real and formidable to themselves.

Now it ought to be evident to all, that if a man is really led of the Spirit he cannot be lawless, in a bad sense. For God is the author of law. Jesus, Himself, said: "Render, therefore, unto Cæsar the things which are Cæsar's and unto God the things which are God's." If, then, the Holy Spirit should lead an individual into lawless acts, the Godhead would be divided against itself and could not stand. This must be admitted as self-evident.

From this it will be seen that Divine guidance cannot **be connected** with lawlessness, only when the name is **used to denominate** what is not Divine guidance, that **is, the objection** really has to do with what is not Divine guidance, **but a** spurious form thereof.

But, **asks** the objector, does not this false doctrine **naturally spring** up where the true doctrine is emphasized? This looks plausible, but a little close consideration will suffice to dismiss all such fears.

It is quite true, that if there were no such thing as Divine guidance, there would be no imitations. This is true of every genuine blessing connected with revelation. Hence the simple fact that it is a part of revealed truth accounts for the counterfeits, just as spurious religions owe their origin to the fact that there is such a thing as true religion. But for the fact of its being a part of God's revealed will to His creature man we are not accountable, **and,** therefore, however we may emphasize this truth, or strive to profit by it, we still are unaccountable for others' abuse of it. These abuses, we maintain, are as likely to abound where none seek to secure the full benefits of the doctrine as where some do, nay, more so. Indeed, we claim that it is a self-evident truth, that the greater the number who are really led of the Spirit into all truth the less will be the number of counterfeits, and the greater the facilities for detecting them when they exist.

But whilst this chain of argument should tend to allay any fears in the direction of lawlessness as the direct or indirect outcome of emphasizing this truth in teaching or illustrating it in actual life, there are certain guards against this very thing which are, as we have seen, a part of the subject itself, which, when kept in mind, ought to forever prevent all fears in this direction.

The fact that the very object or design of the guidance of the Spirit is to enable man to fulfil the righteousness of the law (see Rom. viii.), should lead us to suspect that effectual protection against lawlessness lies somewhere in it. And we have this protection in the fact that when the doctrine of Divine guidance is made a scapegoat for sin, that is, when it is put to the front as an excuse for acts which will not bear the close scrutiny of the laws of God and man, in that very act the note of warning is sounded, and, in place of this plea or excuse justifying the act before men, it rather tends to discount it, and awaken the suspicion that the act apologized for or attempted to be justified by this plea, has its origin in self.

Our Saviour calls on His followers to so illustrate

holy living, that, in place of having to bring in the work of the Spirit to explain away or condone apparent wrong doing, men will be so impressed by their lives that they will of necessity connect them with Divine power, and so glorify the common Father which is in Heaven. Therefore we maintain most positively that the doctrine of Divine guidance, as plainly taught in the scriptures, not only cannot be chargeable with lawlessness, in its bad sense, but is the real safeguard against it.

It is true that, in one sense, the Bible teaches lawlessness. But this is, as in former chapters has been fully brought out, simply exchanging attempted obedience to many rules and regulations for perfect obedience to one living law, the ever-present Guide Divine. But, as we have already shown, this latter obedience necessarily secures obedience to all righteous laws, for, "the *righteousness* of the law is fulfilled in us who walk not after the flesh, but after the Spirit."

DANGERS.—It is objected by some that the whole subject is so beset with dangers that it is better to avoid it altogether. For, say they, the whole stream of modern history is lined with wrecks caused by the effort to master this subject.

Strange that this should be affirmed of such a central truth of the gospel. Is it not the boast of all that the very simplicity of the religion of Christ is one of its best recommendations? Can this simplicity argument be a proper one to use if such perils abound in the very heart of Christ's spiritual kingdom? The poet Alexander Pope gives this advice to all concerning secular knowledge—

> "A little learning is a dangerous thing,
> Drink deep or taste not the Pierian spring."

But this objection would make deep draughts from the fountain of spiritual knowledge and constitute the real danger, whilst a smattering of knowledge would secure safety.

This is a startling thought and yet there are not wanting those of reputed eminence amongst men who stand sponsors for it.

But whilst as a surface thought to merely state it is to see its defects and its weakness as an objection, nevertheless, it has its foundation deeper than at first appears.

Those who have made a study of religious biographies will have noticed how an air of mystery runs through most of it concerning the work of the Spirit. Continually incidents in the lives of the most eminent saints are mentioned about which there is a mysterious something that is left unexplained.

Take for illustration the life of that saintly co-laborer of the Wesleys, Thomas Walsh. It is related of him that during his last sickness he was in great spiritual darkness. This phenomenon lasted till just a little before his death, when suddenly the spell was broken, and he departed this life in spiritual rapture and joy. All the Methodist societies were thrown into a species of consternation over this strange experience of the great Irish evangelist, and much prayer was made in his behalf. So when at length he passed out from under this dark cloud into his former bright, sunny experience, corresponding joy was evinced by all.

But mark, no really satisfactory reason was given to

account for this peculiar experience, although many undertook the task. John Wesley gave it as his opinion that it was a kind of spiritual punishment meted out to him for the sin of using his voice too freely, that is, speaking unnecessarily loud when preaching. The only value of this strange deliverance of the Father of Methodism is, that it illustrates the tendency at that time to regard the Holy Spirit in His work as having some human frailties which rendered Him somewhat sensitive to slights, and inclined to be implacable when once offended.

We shall not be surprised if many will regard this opinion as more fanciful than true to facts. However, it did not come to us as a fancy but as the result of close study of the biographies of the eminent saints of past generations. Moreover, this thought, the outcome of such study, became an important factor in our religious history, and so shrouded the whole subject of the Spirit's work on the hearts of believers with mystery and dread, as to stand connected with much serious loss of spiritual blessing on our part, and as requiring great effort to break away from the shadowy fear engendered thereby.

Now we have satisfied ourselves that this nameless dread, the unconscious result of perusing the very best religious biographies, is the true foundation of the objection we are considering.

The only antidote to these fears is the scriptural study of the character of the Holy Spirit. For it will be found that Christ, as portrayed in the Bible, is the true representative to man of the character of God the Holy Ghost as well as of God the Father, and that therefore in patience, in long-suffering, in condescension, in painstaking guidance, and in forgiveness of all forms of disobedience and unbelief He is the exact counterpart of Father and Son.

True it is that, in the best interests of man, the special work of the Holy Ghost is guarded by peculiar laws, even as the manifested presence of God was jealously guarded under the old dispensation. But with this special legislation Christ is as distinctly identified as the Spirit, and it in no wise renders the cultivation of acquaintanceship with the third person of the Trinity more dangerous than with the second.

Certainly we do not wish to minify the serious fact that God, in the person of Christ, has denounced special penalties for slighting or diabolizing the manifested work of the Spirit amongst men. For this work of the Spirit is the great hope of the world, and it is better that some perish in their determined hostility thereto than that the many should fail to be blessed thereby. The whole subject is one of warning to all against attributing any manifested work of the Spirit, no matter what form it may take, or however surrounded and obscured by the crudities of men, to the devil. For after reading Christ's comments on such conduct, it may well be feared that the day of probation immediately closes upon all such.

But this is quite another matter from what we are discussing, for this danger does in no wise threaten the sincere seeker after truth concerning the extent and practicability of Divine guidance.

Such honest seekers may forever dismiss all fears of danger as they do the shadowy forms with which imagination sometimes peoples the region of mists and semi-darkness. As when the clear light of the sun appears, mists and darkness and hobgoblin forms flee away, so, before the simple teaching of Jesus, "the light of the world," all these fears and presumed dangers disappear, and man learns to come into the presence of the Holy Spirit without dread, and soon accepts Him as his most intimate, confidential friend, and then goes forth in His company, comforted with all Divine comforts, and guided easily, naturally into all truth.

But if one enjoying such delightful relations with the Spirit should unwittingly grieve Him, what then ? We reply, that the way to renewed forgiveness and confidential relations is as freely open as is the way of return to Christ. For after a thousand falls He, the Holy One, is as ready to help to his feet the fallen one and encourage him to continue the fight of faith as ever He was at the commencement of the Christian life. Nothing but want of knowledge concerning the true scriptural description of the character of the Holy Spirit can account to us for such incidents as that mentioned concerning Thomas Walsh and the comments made on them. Hence we unhesitatingly pronounce upon this "danger" objection as being founded entirely on ignorance of the true scriptural character of the Blessed Spirit.

UNCHRISTIANIZING OTHERS.—But, asks another objector, Will not the acceptance of the doctrine of Divine guidance after this unconditional manner unchristianize all who have not in the past or do not now or in all the future so accept it ?

Our Lord has met this objection and answered it satisfactorily in the passage which reads: "And that servant, which knew his lord's will, and made not ready, nor did according to his will, shall be beaten with many stripes; but he that knew not and did things worthy of stripes, shall be beaten with few stripes: And to whomsoever much is given, of him shall much be required: and to whom they commit much, of him will they ask the more."—Luke xii. 47, 48.

Herein is contained the principle of just judgment concerning all. It evidently teaches that failure to walk in all the light of truth possible under the circumstances accounts one worthy of punishment, and that just as the advantages of increased light are positive to him who accepts that increased light, so the loss or punishment is increased to him who still rejects.

Love of the truth and eager desire to discover it and use it when known, Jesus declared to be the necessary qualification of His followers. "This is the judgment, that the light is come into the world, and men loved the darkness rather than the light; for their works were evil. 'For every one that doeth ill hateth the light, and cometh not to the light, lest his works should be reproved. But he that doeth the truth cometh to the light, that his works may be made manifest, that they have been wrought in God."—John iii. 19-21.

Now there is no safer inference from this teaching of Christ than this, that whether in the darkness of heathenism, in the glimmering light of Mohammedanism, the twilight of Greek or Romish churches, or in the varying intensity of light in the different branches of Protestantism, he who meets these conditions of the Saviour, and is an earnest seeker after spiritual light, always appropriating it when found, no matter what his failures may be, cannot come under condemnation.

But who, we ask, beside the great searcher of all hearts, can decide concerning this attitude of any man towards spiritual truth?

The individual who to-day turns away from any additional light because, forsooth, it might prove an inconvenience, or a source of condemnation, would, in all likelihood, have rejected Christ on the same grounds if he had lived in His day. The principle which underlies the acceptance or rejection of any spiritual truth is exactly the same, whether that truth comes to us through the living Christ Himself, through an apostle, or through one of His most illiterate, uncouth or despised followers.

We have every reason to suppose that John Wesley was an honest searcher after spiritual truth, when with his well-read Bible in his hand he yet failed to discover the doctrine of the witness of the Spirit. And he simply illustrated this attitude of his soul when the additional light came to him in the person of the humble Moravian missionary, for he eagerly embraced the light and thenceforth walked in its brightness.

To maintain that John Wesley, before that epoch in his history, was not a true and accepted follower of the Lord Jesus Christ would outrage every notion of justice and propriety which God has implanted in the heart of man, and would make loving, loyal obedience to the great Captain of our salvation an utter impossibility.

Peter gladly recognized this truth when sent to preach the full Pentecostal gospel to the Gentiles as represented by Cornelius and his friends, exclaiming: "Of a truth I perceive that God is no respecter of persons; but in every nation he that feareth Him, and worketh righteousness, is acceptable to Him."—Acts x. 34, 35.

Evidently then in Christ's kingdom it is not so much success in obtaining light as the attitude of the soul towards spiritual light, that is regarded.

Hence our answer to the objection now under consideration is that the acceptance or rejection of the doctrine of Divine guidance in its fullest measure only affects the individual so accepting or rejecting. If to any one it comes as a clear call from God to increased privilege in the gospel, to such and only to such the preaching of the gospel is a savor of life unto life or of death unto death.

As to our judgment of others, we know of no safe rule whereby we may know concerning their attitude to the doctrine whether it is that of love for, hatred to, or indifference for the truth.

True it is that God by His Spirit may make exceptional cases, and communicate to individuals knowledge concerning the soul condition of some for the benefit of all concerned. But these exceptional cases, as illustrated in the lives of the apostles, only proved the absence of any general law concerning this matter.

We therefore maintain that in propagating this Pentecostal truth, whether by lip or pen or life, we need be fettered by no fears of uncharitable judgment concerning others as the legitimate outcome.

A CHECK TO INDUSTRY.—Some objectors maintain that the doctrine of Divine guidance, taught after this full manner, would tend to check patient labor in every direction. For instance, say they, why apply the intellect to the solution of any difficult problem? Why not expect to be led supernaturally into the desired knowledge?

We answer that such objections imply that the Holy Spirit may be regarded as a servant and not necessarily always as an absolute sovereign.

Divine guidance may at one time be as complete where one is called to patient, painstaking effort in the discovery of a truth as when, at another time, a truth is given as a species of intuition. But in any case we may rest assured that where patient labor is the best for all concerned then that will be the manner of Divine guidance.

There is no intimation given anywhere that he who accepts the Holy Spirit as guide into all truth will at once revel in all the intellectual pleasures of a Newton, or even be as conversant as a Luther or a Calvin in dogmatic theology, or that he will escape labor and sorrow—the double curse connected with Adam's sin. But whilst it is true that still like our Master we may grow weary and foot-sore by the length of the journey and would fain sit down by some wayside resting place, that it will ever and anon be in order, because of the sorrows and afflictions of life, to utter the prayer, "If it be possible let this cup pass from me," nevertheless in the very midst of such weariness the heaven-born opportunity to instruct some Samaritan stranger will cause us to forget both hunger and weariness, and in the very shadow of our cross we can, like our great Captain, speak of our joy being full.

We repeat a thought, elsewhere expressed, that the Holy Spirit will in all labors with the human soul work in perfect harmony with the laws of nature, that is, with the laws of God. Now as all sacred history proves that miracles or apparent opposition to the known laws of mind and matter has only been an occasional incident in God's dealings with individuals or nations, so after this manner believe He will still continue to manifest Himself to man. Wherever miracle is to the advantage of him who is led of the Spirit, all things considered, it shall not be wanting. But whether in harmony with, or in apparent opposition to, God's general laws concerning mind and matter, he who walks with God and claims by faith the spiritual completeness of the present dispensation shall know the perfect will of God concerning him, and shall be able to do that will fully. For thus has God ordained it for His own glory and the happiness of His creature—man.

CHAPTER XXVII.

LIVING TESTIMONY.

DEEMING it to be in full agreement with the practical design of this volume, we propose to present to our readers the experiences of a few living illustrations of the practicability and advantages of the doctrine of *Divine Guidance*.

As we have woven our own personal experience into the very texture of the book itself, we do not think it needful to repeat it in this concluding chapter. We have selected these witnesses, of design, from different walks in active life. Whilst some are at present engaged in ministerial work, others are in business life, some having attained considerable prominence therein; still others adorn the less public walks of life.

It is due to all of them to say that we simply intimated to them, mostly by letter, our intention of publishing a book on Divine Guidance, with the request that they would assist to the extent of their personal experience. We fully appreciated the serious nature of the request we made, and are correspondingly gratified by the cheerful response.

The reader can easily understand by a process of self-questioning, what it means to be asked to write out a personal Christian experience to be placed before the public in book form. But at the same time it will be difficult to conceive of any motive other than the love of Christ constraining, as strong enough to secure the result.

We grant that some shallow natures can be acted on by a simple love of notoriety. But we maintain that in every such instance there are not wanting other incidents in such lives to show that they are more or less erratic. But in the case of all these witnesses we have yet to hear of the first charge, from friend or foe, which tends to class one of them with extremists in any one thing save only in the matter of Divine guidance.

THE CHRISTIAN EXPERIENCE OF REV. B. SHERLOCK.

I was brought up in an intensely religious household. Family devotion, religious conversation, moral culture and restraint, backed up by righteous living, furnish the salient things in the picture which memory shows of the days of my childhood, and indeed all the years of my home-life.

At the age of fifteen I was converted, and in a few years afterwards, mainly through the reading of the life of Carvosso, I was moved to seek with whole-hearted earnestness for the blessing of perfect love, which I received after some hours of determined pleading. God is love, and He will not turn any empty away who seek from Him with sincere importunity that which will make them more like Him.

Why it was, that the glow and the glory of that experience remained with me only for a few days, it might not profit the reader to tell, even if one could be specific as to the principal cause. The experience was new to me, and there was no one among those that surrounded me who definitely professed the experience. If there had been, possibly I might have regained it immediately after the first shadow that came upon its brilliance, as a consequence of a disobedience resulting from a yielding to self in the form of constitutional timidity. But I blame no one.

The years that followed were years of very little satisfaction of soul: declensions and revivings, resolutions made in great sincerity, and broken, partly because they did not go far enough at the start, but really because resolutions to do better are not, *in themselves*, any part of God's programme of righteousness for this dispensation.

Ten years after my conversion I came to Canada, and in one year afterwards entered the Methodist ministry. The question of Holiness, or Entire Sanctification as it is understood by the Methodists, came before my conscience from time to time, especially at camp-meetings or other times of religious excitement, when I would be found on my knees pleading for the restoration of the lost experience, but between these seasons it invariably faded away.

The blessing was apparently grasped and held for some short period, more than once during the course of some twenty-two years of ministerial life. It was generally held while engaged in active "revival" work, but faded away after such special seasons ceased.

About eleven years ago, during a season of enforced

leisure, I took hold more firmly and earnestly on God, and then wrote a series of letters which were published in the "Christian Guardian" of Toronto, Ont., on "Hindrances to Holiness" and "What Holiness is and how to be holy," for which I have been thanked by more than one reader.

In about a year afterwards the Canada Holiness Association was formed, including me as one of its first members. We started consciously on the mental platform occupied by Wesley, Fletcher, Clarke and others of the fathers of Methodism on this subject, which is substantially the same as that on which the leaders of the modern holiness movement in England, and especially the United States, have stood and do now stand.

We honestly thought at that time, that the methods of work, and mode of presenting the subject which had been adopted and used by the late Mrs. Palmer, Dr. Foster, Bro. Inskip and others, were as nearly right as possible. But after a few years our President, Rev. N. Burns, began to see that the Holy Spirit of God was not receiving due honor and recognition, neither by us, nor by the Church generally. His teachings on this line, given with that calm boldness, which comes of intense conviction of their truth, sometimes startled me as well as others; and but for the fact that I was not perfectly satisfied with my own experiences, might have produced the result in my case that they did in some others, that of driving me from the association.

The remark of Joseph Agar Beet in his little book on " Holiness as taught by the writers of the Bible," when speaking of the work of the Holy Spirit he says, " All other influences tend away from God," came up again and again, suggesting the correlative truth, that the Holy Spirit is the sole cause of Christian holiness. If therefore, I reasoned, I have not sufficiently studied this subject, and it appears that Bro. Burns has studied it at least more than I have, then I am not in a position to object to his teachings until I do so understand it as to be sure of my ground.

About three years ago or more while meditating on this subject, the thought came to me with almost the precision and impression of a voice speaking to the outward ear: "You and the Church generally have been baptized into the name of the Holy Ghost, as truly as into the name of the Father and the Son, but neither you nor the Church in general have given Him equal honor and recognition with the Father and the Son." From that moment I began to acknowledge personally and publicly, His personality, His indispensableness, and His true Deity, as the truth became more and more vividly evident to me.

Soon the guidance of the Spirit was seen to be a specialty in Christ's plan; and that, with all that Jesus teaches concerning Him, was heartily accepted. Having thus broken loose from the standpoint of former years, I saw and continue to see with ever-increasing clearness and certainty, that the Holy Spirit of God is the sole cause of all holiness; that as His "strivings" produce conviction of sin, and as when He is yielded to in those strivings he produces the new birth, so the fulness of the Spirit as that fulness was bestowed on the day of Pentecost, fulfilling the Saviour's own promise, is the only "second blessing" that He, the Saviour, has promised. And accordingly in my own dealings with God, and in my preaching to the Church I do not speak of the "blessing" of holiness, or the "state" of entire sanctification as finalities to be grasped and held, but rather open my own heart and keep it open, to be "filled with the Spirit," being satisfied that the holiness which He produces must be what pleases God, and I press it upon others in the same way; as I see that that is Christ's way of promising and of bestowing. I now have complete, radiant satisfaction of soul, from moment to moment, from month to month; and have seen more success in my ministry in the "perfecting of the saints," both as to numbers and quality, than ever before.

As to the guidance of the Spirit, His teaching, His taking the things of Christ and shewing them to the believer, His bringing all Christian things to his remembrance, His glorifying Christ, His showing things to come, His giving power, all of which are definitely promised by the Master—I have accepted Him, the Comforter, to do all these things for me, or in me, and have had experience of every one of these benefits.

I have been guided to the advantageous purchase of needed matters for life and comfort, in the purchase of a horse; in the choice of the best road to travel when I had no knowledge of what was ahead of me; guided in pastoral visitation to the places and persons where I could do the most good.

I am constantly guided in the choice of subjects to preach from; sometimes guided away from previous preparation, and given a different message to deliver.

It is not by any means the rule with me that I preach a different theme from what has been previously thought of and prayed over; but it seems as if He allows me occasionally to "prepare" something that He does not intend that I shall preach, in order to teach me His sovereignty in His own sphere. I have seen as much proof that the right subject was taken on such occasions (to say the least) as when He shewed me previously the subject to deliver. At such times the invigoration of my Christian memory has been a surprise to myself. The guidings I have experienced have been to me a demonstration, as strong and definite as anything can be, that they were Divine. For I have been led to ends that could not have been foreseen by the keenest human shrewdness, taking step after step, not knowing what the consequences would be, but all the while happy because I was *sure* that the result would be the very best possible for me at the time. . And as of myself I could not be certain that my notions of what is right or wrong would always be perfectly correct, and remembering that my Saviour said, "He shall teach you all things," I gladly avail myself of His teaching. And as to what is meant by "He shall take of mine [Christ's] and show it unto you," that is better realized than I can describe. Lessons that the letter itself cannot teach, lessons never found in lexicon or commentary or homiletical review, not found in "the words which man's wisdom teacheth." These guidings and teachings do not come by chance or coincidence, for they are asked for by me, asked in implicit faith, because my Saviour promised them and I cannot do without them and call myself a believer in

His word. I dare not insult Him by ignoring his definite offer of such priceless and undeserved benefits.

An increasing number of Christians have been led under my ministry of late to believe, and receive, and live as above described; and they every one declare, that their previous doubts and difficulties about the Christian life no longer exist; "that the law of the Spirit of life "in Christ Jesus hath made them free from the law of "sin and death," and that "the righteousness of the law "is fulfilled in them, who walk not after the flesh but "after the Spirit."

Arkwright, Ont.

CHRISTIAN EXPERIENCE OF ISAAC ANDERSON.

It is no small undertaking to write an experience covering nearly half a century, so as not to become tedious to the reader. But by the help of my "Guide Divine" I will endeavor to cover the ground briefly and to the best of my ability

Right here let me suggest, dear reader, that if I should happen to record some items of little interest to you, kindly remember that they may be of infinite importance to others. The object of the writer is simply to help such as are *earnestly* seeking the *Rest of faith*, and are willing, yes, anxious to pay the price, viz., to make an "*utter, glad, irreversible* surrender" of their whole being to God the Holy Ghost—that other Comforter and guide into all truth whom Jesus promised and *hath sent*.

I will now ask the reader to go with me to the place

of my birth, which event occurred in the year 1841, on a farm about four miles east of the town of Galt, in the township of Beverley. My parents were by no means wealthy; our house was built of logs, and contained *all of two rooms*. My father died when I was eight years old, the first sad event of my life. From the age of ten years I had to work hard, late and early, and received but little of this world's goods in return. A "hickory" shirt, blue jean pants and smock, a straw hat, my feet washed and I was dressed for Sunday. My education was crowded into a few years at a country school, with a vacation at hard labor, commencing about the time the snow left in the spring and continuing while there was anything to be done on the farm—about the time old Earth put on her white robe again. Our family consisted, at that time, of eight—five boys and three girls; I was number five. The death of my youngest brother, a dear little curly-haired boy, along with the death of my father, led to my first serious thoughts about God, heaven and my immortal soul, and resulted in my first effort to live a Christian life.

This was a hard and fruitless struggle, for indeed I was about the only member of our family who, at that time, made any such attempt, and my notions as to how to succeed were very crude. I may say there was no success beyond the first impressions, which God Himself had planted and which never have been erased.

I do not think I ever saw the inside of a church till I was about 13 years of age, an event which stands connected in my life with the first time I was induced by the pressure of circumstances to face the wide, wide world for myself.

In my removal I had no use for either a "Saratoga" or an express wagon! I spent my first summer in the employment of a neighboring farmer, who paid me the large sum of $5 per month. But to me every dollar of that money was worth one hundred cents, for, although only a small boy, I hesitate not to say I did the work of an average man.

My next move was to the town of Galt, where I engaged with a firm to learn the grocery business, at a salary for the first year of $35, board and washing thrown in, and from 7 o'clock in the morning till 9, 10, 11 and sometimes 12 at night, I accomplished as much work in delivering goods with a wheelbarrow as the boy of to-day does with a horse and wagon.

About two years later found me up in the wild woods of Michigan, where a part of our family had found a new home, and where my assistance seemed to be a necessity in order to keep the "wolf from the door." This was accomplished by dint of long hours of unceasing toil.

A load of shingles was known in that country as a "grist." I knew what it was, many a day, to shave shingles until my right hand every morning would refuse to obey my will, and so I would open it with my left hand and place the handle of my knife in it, then like a foundered horse I would gradually warm up and so perform another and another day's labor.

I spent one winter in the lumber woods, driving teams, up at four or five in the morning and busy till ten at night. How well I remember the shortness of those nights! it seemed to me that both ends met just when I was called.

About the year 1859 found me back again in my native town (Galt), where, in the following year, I was converted to God. But it was not without a conflict, fierce and long, that I obtained converting grace. Under the terrible strain my health began to fail, ending in sickness almost unto death; and well I remember how welcome death would have been had I known that my peace was made with God, and how, at the end of three weeks of most terrible suffering, I gave up *trying* to believe. I thought, Well, I must die, and I'll just trust it all to Jesus, I can do no more, and then I sank away to rest. I expected to die, and those around me thought I was going. Tired nature went to sleep for the first time during all those terrible days and nights, and such a sleep! I shall never forget it. This event is stamped indelibly upon my mind.

I slowly recovered my health and found my way to the Methodist church, joined a class and began to tell " How great things the Lord had done for me."

It was not long, however, before I found myself again " doing the things that I would not," yes, and " making many crooked steps "—a life of sinning and repenting; sometimes completely backslidden and again restored and rejoicing. I was even used of the Lord to help others, some of whom I doubt not are in heaven long ago and will meet me there in the sweet by-and-by.

In 1866 I had the good fortune to marry one whom I believed to be the best young woman I had ever seen— and I was not disappointed. She proved to be a true Christian and a helpmeet. As time rolled on we found ourselves surrounded with treasures, three sons and three daughters, our home the abode of happiness and sunshine.

About 1870 I embarked in the oil business, which necessitated my removal from Galt to Toronto, the latter place being more suitable as a distributing point. I have continued in this business ever since and Toronto is still my home.

Many were my ups and downs during the next ten years; sometimes failure in business life, as well as in religious, the harrowing details of which prudence forbids me to impose upon the reader. Suffice it to say, that on the first Sunday morning of 1880, after reviewing all my past life I found it to be in the truest sense most unsatisfactory both commercially and religiously, and right there I closed up the book of the past, writing failure upon every page, and while listening to a sermon in old Bloor Street Methodist Church, delivered by Rev. Dr. Hunter, from the text " From this day will I bless you," Haggai ii. 19, by God's help I made a fresh start, opened a new book and began a new life.

I know and God knew in that memorable hour that I counted not my life dear that I might win Christ. At once I realized that God spoke to me through the text. He meant me. It was for me, and I walked out upon it. It has borne me up for over nine years, during which time I have been writing victory instead of failure.

A few days after my restoration to God's favor and smile, while listening to the testimony of a good brother, who is now in Ireland, who professed to enjoy the blessing of holiness, I discovered there was higher ground for me. True to my promise made to God I at once accepted all I knew to be for me, which was a life after the " perpetual cleansing " sort, and a vast improvement over all former experiences. Herein I greatly rejoiced, and grew in grace and knowledge, carrying everything to God in prayer. I soon found improvement and success in business, and victory over the "besetting sins" of the past, and, laying aside "every weight," I soon found myself *running* in the way of His commandments with pleasure and delight.

God greatly blessed to me the reading of Joseph Cook's lectures on "Orthodoxy," "Conscience," and other subjects about that time, through which I was helped out of many theological difficulties. I shall ever be thankful for the productions of this truly great man, whose business it is to harmonize religion and science, and to teach men how to think. I found myself intensely in love with the truth, and delighted in fellowship with all who were like-minded and able to shed new light upon my pathway.

Among the difficulties that presented themselves to my mind was the difference between justification and sanctification. I confess that for years I failed to find what to me was a satisfactory solution of this question, and so I had to be content to wait. But in due course of time help came.

It pleased God to send to our city the Rev. N. Burns, president of the Canada Holiness Association, with whom it has been my privilege to become most intimately acquainted and associated. He was the first person whom I had ever met who professed and enjoyed the baptism of the Holy Ghost in Pentecostal fulness and power. To me it was only necessary to behold new light to possess it and so I embraced my Comforter and guide Divine as lightgiver, inspirer and guide into all truth—in short, as the one law of my being, and so came an end to this vexed question: and here let me say was the entrance into the land of settled questions. I saw that in order to *live* a *justified* life it was needful to *be filled with the Spirit.*

I had been for some time the recognized leader of the only Holiness meeting held in Toronto in those days. The attendance was small, and those who professed and enjoyed the blessing of Holiness, as it was then taught and lived, would have been fully represented by the fingers upon one hand; and for some time after the advent of Bro. Burns in our city, there seemed to be but little progress. After a time, his teaching on Divine guidance brought down a shower of opposition from sources where it was least expected. But right in the midst of the conflict came victory, and ere long a goodly number entered into the grand experience of Pentecostal life.

But to return to my personal experience, the greatest of all problems to be solved was, how to live a *holy business life.* Previous to my acceptance of the Holy Spirit as my one law and guide, I attempted to accomplish it by laying down certain rules and regulations; but in spite of every effort I failed to keep them, and so I was really condemned by the teaching of Christ and His apostles: "Did not Moses give you the law, and yet none of you doeth the law?"—John vii. 19. "For whosoever shall keep the whole law, and yet stumble in one point, he is become guilty of all."—James ii. 10.

But on the other hand, who will deny that Jesus required—demanded of *all* who would be His disciples, that they should *keep His commandments* and *do God's will on earth as it is done in heaven?* Did our Saviour mean what He said? Did He demand the impossible? Surely no one dare charge Him with insincerity, or unreasonableness! We are forced then to believe that it is possible to " walk worthy of God unto all pleasing," and we read of no exceptions. " God is no respecter of persons," the business man's life must then be included. So I could no longer say, as is said by some, " Religion is religion and business is business "; no, no, to the true disciple everything is sacred. " Whether, therefore, ye eat or drink, or whatsoever ye do, do all to the glory of God."—1 Cor. x. 31. There must, therefore, be *some way* to live a life that pleases God in *all* things.

Now, must I be branded as a " fanatic," as an " egotist," as " self-righteous," when I say that I have found the secret of living such a life, and proclaim to the world that it is possible—yes, it is *gloriously* possible, abundantly and delightfully possible; embracing all the thoughts, words, actions and transactions of a business life? or do I hear the reader say, Praise God for such possibilities! and earnestly and anxiously enquire, *How may I* know this secret, that I too may live this life?

Assuming that I hear the enquiry from an honest heart, filled with intensest and purest purpose and determination at all costs to embrace this secret, remembering, too, that " the secret of God is with them that fear Him," from the gladness of my heart, overflowing with love and praise to Him who hath redeemed and cleansed me from my sins in His own most precious blood, I will tell you the secret. It is all in the promise of the Father—the gift of the *Holy Ghost*, that other Comforter of whom our Lord Jesus spake, when He said: "If I go away I will send you another Comforter, even the Spirit of truth," "He shall abide with you," "He shall guide you into *all* truth." "He shall bring all things to your remembrance," "He shall teach you all things." Reader—Brother, He has come! He came to the one hundred and twenty in the upper room at Jerusalem. In His power, immediately thereafter, Peter preached and three thousand were converted, and they, too, at once received Him. Read the records for yourself and see if it was not the normal experience of the early Christians, to receive the Holy Ghost. And in all subsequent ages men of might and power, whose lives have stood out in bold relief, who have left their footprints on the sands of time, never to be erased—whose lives still live and shall continue to live a benediction to humanity—were men filled with the Holy Ghost. Yes, He has come, come to me; I have embraced Him. He abides with me—the continued life of my beloved Saviour, with me! He is all that was promised He should be, to me:

> "In sorrow He's my comfort,
> In trouble He's my stay;
> He tells me every care on Him to roll;
> He's the Lily of the Valley,
> The bright and Morning Star;
> He's the fairest of ten thousand to my soul."

The yoke of Jesus *is* easy, His burden *is* light. It is easier to do business by telling the truth and being straightforward, than it is to do it any other way. Yes, I can say all I ought to say and say no more, and carry with me every moment the "Well done" of my Heavenly Father; so, instead of a never-ending uncertainty and doubt as to whether I am pursuing the right course, it is mine to enjoy the sweet rest of faith and happy conscientiousness that God is working in me both to will and to do of His good pleasure. His will has become my glad choice and preference, and so I can say, "I delight to do thy will, O God": "we who have believed *do* enter into rest."

I go about my business duties with as much delight and abounding joy as the school boy goes to play ball. If prosperity and success attend my labors, I praise God. If reverses and losses come (and they do come), I praise God. To me it all means *success*, for my God has said that all things shall work together for good to them that love Him, and that means me.

With all unnecessary care and worry thrown off, I am free to use all the powers of mind and body in the right and necessary direction, and so can accomplish vastly more with greater ease than at any former period of my life. I can do more business, more Christian work, and have more time for recreation than I ever had under other circumstances; truly "Godliness *is* profitable unto *all* things."

I come now to my latest and greatest of all trials, viz., the death of my precious wife, who very recently left me for the other shore, after having shared my joys and sorrows for the past twenty-three years. Mine was no ordinary loss. Few men are blest with partners of truest worth—the embodiment of all that constitutes the noblest of wives and best of mothers. She lived only for the comfort and well-being of others, and filled our home with the sunshine of her most truly Christ-like life; always comforting those around her with the comfort wherewith she herself was comforted in the Holy Spirit. Of us it could most truthfully be said: "they twain were *one* flesh—one in heart and life, one in Christ Jesus." I have made this reference to the life of the dear departed one that the reader may the better appreciate my great loss. Only those, however, who know from experience what it is to lose such a treasure, can enter into my experience; it cannot be explained to others. I knew for months previous to her death that she could not live, and know full well what it means to be "sorrowful yet always rejoicing." To the praise and glory of our God, let me say, His grace was and is sufficient, just as Jesus promised it should be; for by His favor I can say: "The Lord gave and the Lord hath taken away, blessed be the name of the Lord."

Thus I have told you in *some measure* my Christian experience. But finding myself unequal to the task, with Paul I exclaim, "Now unto him that is able to do exceeding abundantly above all that we ask or think according to the power that worketh in us, unto him be glory in the church by Christ Jesus throughout all ages, world without end. Amen."

CHRISTIAN EXPERIENCE OF MRS. McMAHON.

My childhood's home was on the shores of Lake Ontario, and sitting by the window of my room, I spent many an hour watching the lake in its varied moods. It was there I first realized something of the power of the great Unseen, as He managed the waters, sometimes in their billow-crested magnificence, and sometimes in the summer calm when their silvery surface was only eclipsed in loveliness by the delightful hush everywhere, as though there was nothing for the world to do but rest. My childish mind acknowledged this power as God and worshipped Him, my adoration only finding vent in some such words as these, I love the Being who can do such wonderful things, and I generally ended in wishing I knew more about Him. These were the sublime moments of my childhood and the dawning of spiritual knowledge. Then I began to know for myself the Creator as my Father. I say, for myself, for though my parents were Christians and taught me of these things, I only knew them for myself as God revealed Himself to me as Creator in His works.

I cannot remember which I learned first, the story of the cross or the ten commandments, but I do know that with the advent of these came the beginning of spiritual conflict. I know that when I read for the first time the sufferings and shameful death of Christ, my whole being felt sick with the thought that so good a man had been so cruelly used, and I knew from that time I loved the man of sorrows for his unselfish life and martyr death. I believed also what the Bible taught me, that He died that whoever believed in Him would not be lost but have eternal life. I felt that I could claim it all for I believed on Him with all my heart.

But I did not yet realize His power in my daily life

to conquer and subdue all my sinful nature and make me like Himself. How strange it seems that with the light given then I should have had to wade through years of bitter conflict before knowing the rest that remains for the people of God! How like Paul in the 7th of Romans was my life then! when I would do good evil was present with me, the flesh continually at war with the Spirit and often bringing me into captivity, and like him I often felt, O wretched girl that I am, who shall deliver me?

I will now proceed to explain as briefly as I can the nature of this conflict in my life. The ten commandments contained for me God's written law, which if obeyed, seemed to me the ideal life. I believed that Jesus kept that law, and that I ought to, and so the law became my judge.

I had a very strong will, and was in consequence a great source of anxiety to my mother, who wanted prompt obedience and whose authority sometimes chafed me sorely. Often I wilfully disobeyed, and oftener offended ignorantly. But every day brought me into trouble, for I felt it to be impossible to keep the law, and yet after times of wilful disobedience came sorrow and remorse and confession and restoration to the Divine favor. I never had heard of what Methodists call the witness of the Spirit, but I felt that God was pleased and I was in harmony with nature and its God. But when overtaken in a fault through some impulse or ignorance, and then condemned, strange questions arose within me as, Why did God not show me before I did it? How could He accuse me when I did not know? For years such questions as these had no solution, and I wandered in bondage to the law, not knowing that the Spirit sets the captive free and yet enables him to fulfil the righteousness of the law.

In the year 1872 I was married, and as my husband was a member of the Methodist church I also became a member of that body. This step brought me into closer contact with various forms of church work, and I entered into it with much earnestness, but felt in it all a great lack somewhere.

I once picked up a Bible that had been presented to me when a child in Sabbath school, on the fly leaf of which the giver had written the verse, "All scripture is given by inspiration of God, and is profitable for doctrine, for reproof, for correction, for instruction in righteousness; that the man of God might be perfect and thoroughly furnished unto all good works." Here was another enigma. It seemed that the instructions and reproofs were all there, but how should I manage to secure them. I needed so much at the time that I could not just find direction for, and, if I waited till I understood the Word thoroughly, years must pass before I could get the first day's work done just right and according to the scripture plan, and so I lived longing to do the right things, and yet always conscious of failure. Soon the trials of married life came and I was unfit to bear them. I buried one little girl, and had much sickness with my other children, and plenty of financial trouble.

In the year 1882 we moved to Toronto, and three days after buried our second son—a lovely boy of six years.

My cup of sorrow seemed full; but I was enabled through grace to say, "Thy will be done." After this my longings to do God's perfect will were greater than ever before, and consecrations were multiplied.

About this time my attention was specially turned to the work of the Holy Ghost in connection with this dispensation. I was somewhat startled by the number of times His name appeared in the New Testament, and speculated much about Pentecost and the definite experiences concerning receiving Him as a particular gift, but had to admit to myself that I had no clear understanding of the matter.

Not long after this the New Year's consecration service took place in our church. All were invited to stand and renew their consecration. I stood and took the vow with the rest. After going home, despair came upon me as I thought how often I had done the same thing, and as often failed. In my extremity I cried, *Must it always be so?* My Father, is there *no* remedy? Then a voice spoke within me, saying, The remedy is in the Holy Ghost. Christ said that He would send Him to be your guide, teacher and witness—read about him. Again I read of Him, but as I read that time the light within me became as noon, for I understood for the first time that Christ meant that after He went away He and His Father would come back to this world and live in me and show me what to do and when and how. It seemed amazing, wonderful, but there it was, and as I looked back I remembered that all the way along the Spirit had been trying to teach and make me understand His teachings, but now I saw it all; the Holy Ghost had been given at

Pentecost for all the world of believers, and for all time. He was as Peter said, "the Gift." I saw that I must accept Him to be my power to help me do always the right thing at the right time and in the right way. This was just what my being craved, and I hesitated not to appropriate for myself so great a boon. So without any special physical demonstration I received the Holy Ghost, and from that time rest began. I felt sure He would do His part. I just kept trusting, no matter what were my surroundings, and obeying just as He made clear to me what to do. If at any time there came up what appeared to be two things to do I claimed by faith that He would only let me do the right, as He knew I was willing to do either.

What a rest now that the government of my life is on His shoulders! Now He is to me the mighty counsellor, now bondage exists no longer, for He lives with me and helps me to fulfil the law. He shows me that He will teach me, and will not chide me for what I do not know, that I must not expect to know every thing to-day, but learn as a child by the moment or day, that He will give me wisdom and not upbraid because of past ignorance. How like a father, brother, helper, friend, has He become to me. Now indeed has He become my salvation, not only for the life after this, but in the new life where I need saving all the time.

He enables me to walk in the light with Him as He is in the light. Language fails here to describe the joy, the rest, the satisfaction I have obtained. I cannot tell it, it is unspeakable. I know I am changing from glory to glory; I now feel that I am growing, that my life to-day pleases my Master. I have His "Well done" for today, but will know more and do better to-morrow.

> "Now I have found the ground wherein
> Sure my soul's anchor may remain."

CHRISTIAN EXPERIENCE OF REV. ALBERT TRUAX.

My conversion was clear and positive. The fruits of the Spirit appeared at once and I was a soul-helper and a soul-winner from the first. I had many times of refreshing and seasons of ecstatic joy, even so great that on one occasion I prayed God to "stay His hand."

Trouble soon came, however. Being naturally fretful, irritable and despondent, these tendencies soon reappeared, greatly marring my peace and hindering my usefulness.

I shed many tears, fasted and prayed and made thousands of good resolutions, but still I failed and knew not how to succeed.

I heard and read a little about Perfect Love and Full Salvation. Mr. Wesley's writings took firmest hold on my mind, and it was through them chiefly that I became convinced of the truth of the doctrine.

At first the experience seemed afar off, to be attained only by agèd saints after years of seeking. However, after pondering the matter in my mind for some time and getting some help from the Rev. Mr. Teeter, my first superintendent, I determined to follow Mr. Wesley's direction and seek the blessing at once by faith. God honored my faith and I entered into the happy experience, in the month of September, 1882.

It was certainly a great epoch in my life, and for a time I thought the great problem of the Christian life was solved and I would have no more trouble. But, alas! I was doomed to disappointment; perplexities soon beset me on every side.

I was willing, obedient, honest and teachable. My soul responded joyfully to all the known requirements of God, my eye was single to His glory, my conscience quick and tender, and I would rather have died than displease Jesus. It was my meat and drink to do the will of God.

Just here came my difficulty. Could I know the will of God in every case and could I know I performed it in a manner well pleasing to Him? At times I did know; I had the clear witness that all I did was right, that God looked upon me with an approving smile. But how could I have this witness perpetual, constant, abiding? I could not answer; I did not know it was possible, though it seemed so reasonable and necessary that it should be so.

Questions like these would arise: Are you sure you did just right to-day? Did you pray and read your Bible enough? Would you not have preached better if you had studied harder and prayed more? How about your feelings, thoughts and words? Have these all been pleasing to God? Of course I tried to be satisfied with having a pure motive and single eye and doing the best I could. My creed demanded this, but it promised me nothing better, and so far as I knew nobody experienced anything better.

But I could not be quite content, for I found to my bitter sorrow that having a pure motive and doing the very best my sanctified common sense and judgment enabled me to do did not prevent my making some terrible blunders—blunders so great that I wondered how God could allow an honest man to make them. Somehow I could not but believe there was a better, surer way if I could only find it.

God can make even Satan to work out His own purposes, and so He used my very blunders to drive me in very desperation to seek a more excellent way.

It was, I believe, in the year 1884 that I came in contact with the "Canada Holiness Association," at their annual camp meeting at Grimsby Park. There I heard something definite about the Spirit's work as teacher and guide into all truth. At first I stood in great doubt and fear of the whole question. The teaching did seem risky, mystical and even fanatical. I thought it was too nearly allied to the Papal dogma of infallibility, and so expressed myself at a morning meeting. However, I would not judge hastily. I gave the subject much attention during the next three or four years, listening to testimony and reading everything I could find on the subject. One thing was certain, if the doctrine were true it would surely meet my want, so I determined to investigate fully.

I am thankful that, while listening to others, I did not neglect the eloquent pleading of my own soul crying out in its need and hunger for *certain knowledge* of the will of God and for power to "do His will on earth as it is done in heaven." At length, about a year ago, God met me and fully convinced me of the truth. I said, "It is enough, I am convinced. It is my privilege to receive the Holy Ghost in a Pentecostal sense to do for me just what Jesus said He would do—'teach me all things and lead me into all truth.'"

And now came the fight of faith. At first I wanted to *feel* guided, to have some signs given me that I was guided, or I wanted to be guided according to my own notion of guidance. But, no; He would not be servant, but Master. I must not manage Him, but He must have the absolute, undisputed control and management of me. I was not to be the judge of my own feelings, thoughts and conduct, but "He that judgeth me is the Lord." After a few tentative experiments and some failures, I was enabled to accept Him by simple faith as my one and only guide, teacher, comforter, empowerer and law in life; and since that time I have lacked for nothing, but have had sure guidance, teaching, comfort and power according to my needs.

THE CHRISTIAN EXPERIENCE OF J. K. CRANSTON.

During the great revival conducted by Russell and Carrol in Galt in 1869, I was converted to God. From that time I endeavored to live a Christian life. Being young and not receiving clear instruction, I understood but little of the work of the Comforter whom the Saviour promised should be to His redeemed ones an abiding guest, keeper and "guide into all truth."—John xvi. 13.

Leaving home when about 15 years of age, I went to Port Hope and there joined the Presbyterian Church, under the pastorate of the Rev. William Donald. Being desirous of living a true Christian life I attended the various services and Bible classes, and joined the Y. M. C. A. as an active member; with some others I distributed tracts every Sabbath.

Some four years after I secured a situation in Galt and became a member of Knox Church. I here sought to serve my Lord and Master, taking an active interest in Church and Sunday school work.

Leaving Galt, I was for some four years connected

with Knox Church, Woodstock, and then again returned to Galt and engaged in the book and stationery business. I again sought to work for Jesus, whom I loved and endeavored to follow.

During all this time and up till September 4th, 1887, I realized that my experience was not a satisfactory one. I found daily that sin did have dominion over me, that the good I would, I did not and the evil I would not, I too often did. I did not have the power to obtain the victory steadily, so that often I would cry out in agony of soul, " Oh wretched man that I am, who shall deliver me from the body of this death ?"

I looked many times to my various ministers for help, and others who were God's professed children. By listening to their testimony I learned that their experience was similar to my own, and I noticed in their prayers that failure, yes, constant failure, was acknowledged and lamented, and the cry went forth: " Woe is me, for I am undone because I am a man of unclean lips."

I settled down, believing all Christians were alike and that no better experience could be enjoyed here, but heaven would be my home after this mortal body was laid aside, and so I lived in a half-dead state for nineteen years. At times I thought, surely there is a better way and would make enquiries, but all to no purpose, being invariably told that the seventh chapter of Romans described the best, Christian experience in this life.

After returning to Galt, some four years ago, I heard a testimony given by Bro. David Caldwell that sounded new and strange to me. He testified that he had received, not only Jesus as his Saviour but also the Holy Ghost in the Pentecostal sense, and walked in Him, and that where once it had been frequent failure, that he now was enabled by the indwelling Comforter to obtain constant victory over the world, the flesh and the devil, and he declared that sin had not dominion over him while he walked in the Spirit. I was interested, and as he repeatedly gave his warm, glowing testimony and thanked God for His keeping power, I began to watch his life. I made his acquaintance, and for years the principal subject of conversation between us was how victory over sin was to be obtained.

I was blind to the truth, however, and thought he was deceived. But then his life was before me and I looked for evidence of failure there and I found none, so that I was compelled to believe that he had a power I knew nothing about. He said he had entered into rest and his life proved it to me.

I now began to realize that the way of Holiness, spoken of in Isaiah xxxv. 8, 9, 10, was the path that all believers had the privilege of walking in while yet on the earth. But how to enter in the way was the question. I became anxious and troubled and the Scriptures were searched daily, and my soul longed for deliverance from the power and dominion of sin; I longed to have the constant smile and approval of God. Beulah Land was before me. I saw the Land, but how to get across Jordan was the difficulty. I met with others who were dwellers in that land, and the fruits of Canaan were exhibited in their joyous, happy lives, and all my desire was to go forward. The situation was examined. I saw that it meant crucifixion and death to self, and a surrender of my will to God in all things, small or great. I saw it meant a consecration without reservation, as in Romans xii. 1—a presenting of myself, body, soul and spirit, unto God, which after all was only a reasonable service. I cried unto the Lord; I tried to die to self, to present myself to Him, but failed. I was in despair, the burden seemed greater than I could bear.

On the 4th September, 1887, Sunday afternoon, Mr. Caldwell and some other friends called and instructed me in the way more perfectly, and explained that by receiving the promised gift, the Comforter, the Spirit of God as a *person* into my heart, He would enable me to be more than a conqueror over the world, the flesh and the devil.

Having previously accepted Christ as my saviour, I

now received the Comforter divine as my empowerer, joy and guide into all truth; yielding myself with all my ransomed powers to God, I entered into an everlasting covenant to allow Him to work in me to will and to do of His own good pleasure, and, come what might, I was the Lord's and His alone, to do whatsoever He commanded me. I arose from my knees but did not experience any change of feeling; but what was better I had a conscious knowledge that I had honestly given myself and all my possessions to God, and that He had accepted me. I had nothing of my own left and I was willing to do anything or be used by Him as He saw fit.

The dear Lord whispered loving and tender messages to me and the joy of the Lord soon flowed like a river into my soul. The love of God was shed abroad in my heart by the Holy Ghost given unto me, a deep settled peace was mine. At last, at last, I cried, I am at rest, and I shall go no more out for ever. "Sweet, happy rest!" The land of Beulah was now entered into and the dear Lord communed with me and led me forth to conquer the enemies of the land. I was led up to the Jericho of my life, and soon found that by walking with God the walls of difficulty disappeared and I was enabled to shout victory through the blood of the Lamb.

My past life was reviewed, and the dear Lord asked me, and gave me grace, to make confession and restitution to my fellow-man for hasty and unkind words, actions and deeds that under temptation and provocation I had yielded to.

Having committed my business to the Lord, I was directed to put away and destroy all goods that were of a doubtful character. I debated for a time with reference to certain goods because everybody in the business sold them, and I was soon convinced that God would not allow me to keep them; when I opened my Bible for counsel, Acts v. 1 to 11 was before me and the matter was settled.

I now constantly realized the sweet comforting presence of my Lord and Master. I knew the blessed Spirit was my faithful guide. Enemy after enemy was conquered and my life from this time was and is to-day a joy and a song, because I have my beloved always with me. Temptations, trials and difficulties have ever been increasing, but I prove the scripture true, My grace is sufficient for you, for greater is He that is in you than he that is in the world.

Since entering this life hid with Christ in God and walking in the Spirit, I have learned that it is not impossible to sin, but I also know and have proved that there is no longer any necessity for sinning. Absolute surrender and trust in my Guide makes it possible to obtain uniform victory over every assailant, and enables me to march forward, growing in grace and knowledge daily. I have found that to doubt the presence and leading of my Lord (because of the seeming difficulties of the way, or for any other cause) leaves me exposed to the enemy of my soul, who at once thrusts in darts of sin. I once yielded to discouragement through apparent failure when I thought I had lost all, and it took several days of terrible soul agony to teach me that the only way was to lay aside my doubts and fears and instantly ask forgiveness and yield an unquestioning trust and obedience to my Guide. I have now learnt that if I would be happy in Jesus there is no other way but to trust and obey—being willing to lose all that I may hold sweet fellowship and communion with my Saviour and my God.

The promise of the Lord in Acts i. 8, "Ye shall receive power after that the Holy Ghost is come upon you, and ye shall be witnesses," has been verified. Our home was opened for meetings. Here the Lord's presence has been wonderfully felt. Many saints have been cheered and helped out into a brighter experience, and sinners have been converted to God, and our one desire is that many more may enter into like precious faith, walk in the Spirit, and so find in Jesus a satisfying portion.

www.ingramcontent.com/pod-product-compliance
Lightning Source LLC
Chambersburg PA
CBHW032103220426
43664CB00008B/1119